Walking through **Le Corbusier**

josé baltanás

Walking through **Le Corbusier**

A Tour of His Masterworks

with 377 illustrations, 247 in color

Thames & Hudson

Translated from the Spanish *Le Corbusier. Promenades*
by Matthew Clarke

First published in the United Kingdom in 2005 by
Thames & Hudson Ltd, 181A High Holborn, London WC1V 7QX

www.thamesandhudson.com

First published in 2006 in hardcover in the United States of America by
Thames & Hudson Inc., 500 Fifth Avenue, New York, New York 10110

thamesandhudsonusa.com

British Library Cataloguing-in-Publication Data
A catalogue record for this book is available from the British Library

Library of Congress Catalog Card Number 2004118220

ISBN-13: 978-0-500-51233-3
ISBN-10: 0-500-51233-7

Printed in Spain

contents

Walking Through Le Corbusier

'I draw a character. I make him enter the house; he discovers its volume, the form of the room and, above all, the amount of light coming through the window or the pane of glass. He advances: another volume, another influx of light. After that, another source of light; still further on, a flood of light and shade on the side, etc.' (1)

Architecture as Movement

The drawings that illustrate several of Le Corbusier's projects (such as the Maison Guiette in Antwerp or the Villa Meyer in Paris, both included in the *Oeuvre complète*) have an unusual narrative order that provides – through a sequence of 'shots', moments in time spliced together – a continuous and uninterrupted view of the space.

In effect, the accompanying texts (the architect's 'voiceover') run in parallel with the images to construct a narrative that recalls the language of the cinema or of comic books, by introducing a temporal factor into a spatial dimension, in a way that would be difficult to perceive from a static viewpoint. The chain of visual sensations triggered by progressive movement do, however, allow the space to be fully understood as the fruit of a tense dialogue between geometrical regularity and expressive impulse, between rules and forms – in short, between reason and feeling.

This accompanying of the observer on a hypothetical tour of a building accurately embodies the most significant principle characterizing the avant-garde in the inter-war period: a perception of architecture as movement that runs in parallel with Einstein's scientific theories. Thus, in the Villa Savoye, a paradigm of those years, the building's placement and layout ensure visual continuity between the exterior and interior, between nature and geometry (two constants in Le Corbusier's architectural thinking) by allowing visitors to go right inside the house itself by car, and then, on foot, to rise ceremonially from the ground floor to the roof by means of two elements of vertical communication: a staircase and a ramp.

The steps of the spiral staircase only allow progress in a spasmodic fashion (rise-stop-rise-stop) that seems to always end up at the same point (due to the path of the staircase, which is tightly folded in on itself); the ramp, however, permits an unimpeded ascent that enhances the unfurling of perceptual experiences – a space–time continuum that Le Corbusier took not from the experiments of Cubism but from the traditional architecture of North Africa (*l'espace arabe*), as he himself made clear in his writings:

'Arab architecture provides us with a valuable lesson. It is appreciated on the move, on foot; by walking and moving around, one can see how the architecture's ordering devices unfurl. This principle is opposed to baroque architecture, which is conceived on paper, around a fixed theoretical point. I prefer the teachings of Arab architecture.' (2)

As a result, the ramp becomes a primordial element in the modern perception of space, the fourth dimension inherent in the *promenade architecturale*, a cleansing ritual symbolized by the distinctive washbasin on the ground floor of the Villa Savoye. In this building, the ramp transforms walking into a ritual, dignifying the space, while also metonymically evoking the machine age by introducing the ramp-road into a domestic interior.

Although the building in Poissy exemplifies the architectural promenade, this concept was already apparent in some of Le Corbusier's earlier works. It can be seen in the house he built for his parents in La Chaux-de-Fonds, featured on pages 22–27. Here, the route through the garden to the house's entrance is winding, making it possible to approach and observe the building from various viewpoints. It leads under a bridge, goes up a few steps and runs along the perimeter of the façade before finally reaching the door. All this represents not so much a descriptive exercise, a reassuring and predictable unfolding of spaces, materials and forms, but rather a powerful emotional experience.

Le Corbusier's first use of the ramp is usually associated with the Villa La Roche, built in 1925, where the magnificent collection of Cubist paintings hung on the walls of the main living room demanded a gradual progression, similar to that of a museum or art gallery. The curved wall of this central space gives rise to a ramp that leads to the owner's library, which projects over the living room. The striking effect of this ramp would appear in different configurations in future works. It is found, for example, in La Tourette monastery, in the access bridge, as well as in the taut walkway on the roof that links the main building with the church, and in the lines of the interior ramps.

Although the physical and symbolic importance of the ramp in the aforementioned works and elsewhere should not be underestimated, it in fact took on its primary role as an element of communication in two earlier projects. In the refrigerated slaughterhouses of Challuny, from December 1917, and Garchivy, finished in December 1918 (mentioned in Josep Quetglas's work, *Promenade architecturale* (3)), the movement of livestock from the pens to the abattoir via ramps recalls an age when such constructions were not only widespread but also essential if beasts of burden were to reach their destination.

Le Corbusier went on to use this system of communication in subsequent projects, including the one that was completed after his death, the Heidi Weber Pavilion. In this case, the ramp not only vertically connects the various spaces but also serves as a means to reconcile the building's bold, metallic geometry with its natural surroundings.

Worthy of particular note in this respect is the Visual Arts Center at the University of Harvard, in Cambridge, Massachusetts, a project that was brought to fruition by the Catalan architect Josep Lluís Sert. The ramps used within this art school cross the building to connect both the adjacent streets – symbolizing the necessary relationship between the academic world and society – and the different levels in the interior space, inviting visitors on a wide-ranging journey, a *promenade architecturale* on foot over a cambered surface for cars.

As discussed above, Le Corbusier makes extensive use of drawings to show the themes of a work, a form of intellectual reflection that is projected over time, and which becomes visible from the moment that he first sees a site, then continues to evolve until it reaches formal completion. The recurrent appearances of sketches from widely varying sources and influences in the *Oeuvre complète* are evidence of the architect's enormous curiosity. At the same time, his desire to demonstrate the existence and importance of his visual records would subsequently also serve as the basis for lucid reformulations that would expand upon these early primitive influences.

The status of drawing as a favoured means of communication links Le Corbusier's architecture with his paintings; in fact, both facets sometimes cohabited when he introduced his own pictorial works into some projects, although he always made a clear distinction between the two modes of expression.

Along with drawing, photography was to become another method for conveying the visual features of modern architecture, this time after the buildings were completed. The camera, a mechanical metaphor for the movement of the eye, is a substitute for original experience, zooming in and out to capture striking details, condensing encounters or displaying a building's polyphony of forms. Moreover, the time lapses between photos echo, with great precision, those used in the language of the cinema to tell a story. Le Corbusier saw photography as an expression of the modern age that made it possible to communicate the ordered sequence of a building, in a way similar to a spoken commentary.

Furthermore, photographic images make it possible to freeze time and record that magical moment when light and space become one and the same thing (architecture as 'volumes under light'). The extensive photographic documentation found in the *Oeuvre complète* constitutes nothing less than a series of architectural promenades; sometimes the same work is shown at different points in its construction, or the entire building process is illustrated in successive volumes.

The contents of the *Oeuvre complète* are not the only evidence of the permanent relationship between space and time in Le Corbusier's thinking. Their form also makes this theme explicit, as both their extent (eight volumes) and their presentation – shunning the descriptive vertical format to take on a horizontal narrative format – invite readers on a visual and metaphorical stroll.

Just as he did with his paintings, Le Corbusier also incorporated photographic images into his architecture. As can be seen in the chapter on the Pavillon Suisse (pages 80–95), built in the university district of Paris between 1930 and 1932, the architect put up a series of panels with photos showing enlarged details of plants and animals in the reception of the students' residence.

This gesture of modernity, which presented photos as if they were pieces of a mural, would go on to be misinterpreted, however. As on other occasions, the architect was once again misunderstood in more traditionalist circles (the more obtuse or prejudiced critics discerned the risk of dehumanizing materialism).

Be that as it may, photography and drawing were widely used by Le Corbusier as a means of communication, regardless of the setting; in fact, they play a part in another discipline of similar importance to him: discursive literature, albeit of an intrinsically narrative nature. The many drawings and photographs included in the considerable body of his written works confirm and highlight his themes, while allowing readers (by cropping, enlarging and concentrating on details) a personal interpretation of their meaning. They are, above all, evidence of Le Corbusier's confidence in the spatial-temporal dimension of images.

The languages of drawing, photography and writing all come together in Le Corbusier's creative and instinctive world. They represent different approaches, overlapping or parallel, that embrace, in all their diversity, the complexity of the architect's work – a complexity that is undoubtedly best expressed by Le Corbusier himself.

About This Book

This book is structured around these concerns, as its title shows, encapsulating as it does the underlying concept: a chain of images that describes in narrative form the different spaces that make up each building. This photographic narrative is supported and completed by text and graphics that are closely related to the images, in order to enhance conceptual comprehension and visual unity.

The introductory text for each building gathers together Le Corbusier's reflections and explanations on what is shown (thereby forming part of the 'walk-through'), in order to place decisions in context, dispel uncertainties or add layers of meaning to the photographic images that follow. In addition, this critical assessment is complemented and completed by contributions from the works of other writers.

The selected buildings are arranged chronologically, and include works from both ends of Le Corbusier's career, including the very first, the Villa Fallet (1905–7), and the last, the Heidi Weber Pavilion, finished two years after his death. This approach makes it possible to follow Le Corbusier's creative evolution over the course of his professional life. This evolution is free from any formal or conceptual determinism and is always open to new interpretations, and despite the range and diversity of its sometimes opposing viewpoints, it has an overall coherence that makes it possible to link the two above-mentioned buildings that opened and closed the architect's remarkable working life. The Heidi Weber Pavilion displays the two reference points constantly present in Le Corbusier's work – nature and geometry – and he learned these from his master, L'Eplattenier, during his formative years in La Chaux-de-Fonds. The lessons spent on analytical drawings of organic forms, which would later lead Le Corbusier towards abstraction, are reflected in the sgraffito on the façades of the Villa Fallet (a pictographic synthesis of the forms of the surrounding trees).

The selected buildings also bear witness to the variety of environments and social conditions in which they were set: private initiatives (family homes); public housing (the Unité d'Habitation in Marseilles); institutional commissions (Pavillon Suisse, Kembs-Niffer lock) and religious communities (La Tourette monastery). The distance in time and space between all of these allows us to read them as a narration and to set off on an intellectual and visual architectural journey through them, accompanied by the ever-present voice of Le Corbusier himself.

Sources
(1) Le Corbusier, *Précisions sur un état présent de l'architecture et de l'urbanisme*, Paris, 1960
(2) Le Corbusier, *The Complete Architectural Works, vol. 2, 1929–1934*, London, 1964, p. 24
(3) *WAM*, nº 5 (1996), reprinted in Josep Quetglas, *Artículos de ocasión*, Barcelona, 2004, pp. 205–58

villa fallet

1905–7 la chaux-de-fonds

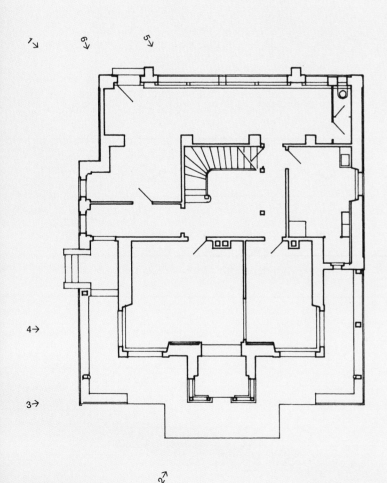

'One more thing. Could you ask one of my classmates, for a fee, to take some good photographs of the house? I have not had time to take them myself. It would be better if they show the exterior, especially the sgraffito in the snow; perhaps when everything is speckled with fresh snow (wall, balcony, etc.) it may have more unity.' (1)

This paragraph from the letter that the young Charles-Édouard Jeanneret sent from Venice to his professor, Charles L'Eplattenier, clearly conveys the close relationship in his mind between architecture and nature, as well as the quest for harmony with local building traditions championed by the master and passed on to his students. This approach was influenced by William Morris's Arts and Crafts movement and the theories of John Ruskin, a staunch defender of a cause-and-effect relationship between architecture and materials, style and construction processes.

L'Eplattenier particularly encouraged his students to deepen their understanding of natural forms by studying their basic structures, thereby bringing together geometry and nature. This process involved long sessions of analytical drawing

Eugène Grasset, motifs from *Méthode de composition ornementale*, vol. 1, 1905

of organic forms and the study of various texts that were then considered essential reading: *The Grammar of Ornament* by Owen Jones (2); *Grammaire des arts du dessin* by Charles Blanc (3); probably *Méthode de composition ornementale* by Eugène Grasset (4), and above all, *The Elements of Drawing* by John Ruskin (5), so much admired by L'Eplattenier. It is important to remember the favourable context in terms of both time and place in which L'Eplattenier gave his classes, as the rich landscapes of the Jura around La Chaux-de-Fonds were matched by the no less powerful expressive intensity of the modernism that held thrall at that time.

The Villa Fallet was built on the northern outskirts of the town, at the foot of the Jura. It was commissioned by Louis Fallet, a jeweller and watch-enameller who was also a member of the board of governors of the local art school and a devoted supporter of L'Eplattenier's innovative teaching methods. In fact, the commission was a result of L'Eplattenier's insistence that Fallet should entrust the design of his new home to Jeanneret.

As Jeanneret obviously had no practical experience, the technical aspects were supervised by a local architect, René Chapallaz, who oversaw the construction and drew up the final plans, while Jeanneret was responsible for the design of the façade and the interior, with the help of other students from his school. In this manner, Charles-Édouard Jeanneret – he only took on the name of Le Corbusier when he was thirty-three – managed to obtain his first architectural commission at the tender age of seventeen.

The house is set on a stone base that compensates for the steep slope of the terrain. The entrance is situated on the highest part of the grounds, to the north, while the main façade faces south, to take advantage of the magnificent, uninterrupted views of the town and valley. The vernacular spirit of the Villa Fallet is evident in the pronounced slopes and overhangs of the roof – which prevent the accumulation of snow while also echoing the form of the nearby trees – and the use of local materials, which allow the house's colour scheme to blend smoothly into its surroundings.

The expressive treatment of these materials – stone, wood, wrought iron and stucco – is inspired by natural forms; the contours of the landscape are reflected in the iron rails on the balconies and the window mullions, as well as in the ornamental sgraffito on the façades and even the supports of the large eaves. Although Jeanneret later distanced himself from this building and the works that followed it, he did acknowledge the careful approach used in the Villa Fallet:

'At seventeen I was lucky enough to meet a man unburdened with prejudices, who ultimately entrusted me with the construction of his house. When I built it – with the greatest possible care and a multitude of (very moving!) details – I was between eighteen and nineteen. That house was probably dreadful, but it was at least uninfluenced by architectural routine.' (6)

Koloman Moser, *Reciprocal Dancers*, plate from the album *Flächenschmuck*, *Die Quelle* series, vol. II, 1901

The ornamental nature of the compositions creates an uninterrupted chain of motifs, like a continuous print, recalling the alternating figure-background perception developed in the *Gestalt* theories of the psychologists of the Vienna School and explored in experimental graphic work by late nineteenth-century artists and designers such as Koloman Moser.

The abundant ornamentation covering almost all the façades of the Villa Fallet
is based on the form of the pine tree – and its branches, cones and needles –
that is typical of the vegetation of the Jura region. These elements are not directly
reproduced, however, but reduced to a strict geometrical figure – sometimes just
a square or triangle – in an attempt to create an autonomous alphabet, subject to
its own rules. This process would later shake off the bonds of naturalism entirely
and enter the realm of abstraction.

The Villa Fallet therefore shows one of the constant elements of Le Corbusier's
thinking and work already in place: his unerring interest in natural forms and,
more specifically, their underlying essential properties. Geometry and nature
would go on to coexist in a fruitful dialogue throughout his career.

Sources
(1) Jean Jenger (ed.), *Le Corbusier. Choix de lettres*, Basel, 2002, p. 40
(2) Owen Jones, *The Grammar of Ornament*, London, 1856
(3) Charles Blanc, *Grammaire des arts du dessin*, Paris, 1867
(4) Eugène Grasset, *Méthode de composition ornementale*, Paris, 1905
(5) John Ruskin, *The Elements of Drawing*, London, 1857
(6) Le Corbusier, *The Complete Architectural Works, vol. 1, 1910–1929*, London, 1964, p. 13

1 View from the north-east, with the entrance on the left. The pronounced overhang and slope of the roofs reflects the need to prevent the accumulation of snow and ice in the harsh conditions of the Jura foothills.

2 Furthermore, these forms blend effortlessly into the lush surroundings, as Jeanneret himself recognized in his letter to L'Eplattenier. The house compensates for the slope of the land with a stone base that also emphasizes the importance of the south façade, which overlooks the valley.

'One more thing: could you ask one of my classmates, for a fee, to take some good photographs of the house? I have not had time to take them myself. It would be better if they show the exterior, especially the sgraffito in the snow; perhaps when everything is speckled with fresh snow (wall, balcony, etc.) it may have more unity.'

3

4

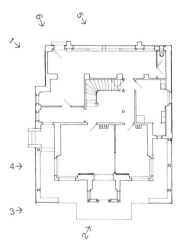

3 and 4 Details of the iron railings on the balconies and the sgraffito on the west façade. Both the materials used – wrought iron, stone, wood, stucco – and the forms they assume – trees, leaves, branches – evoke the surrounding countryside. Slavish imitation is avoided, however, in favour of a pictographic approach that resembles a continuous print of simple geometrical motifs; these form a self-contained vocabulary, no longer connected to the landscape but rooted in its own compositional syntax.

5

6

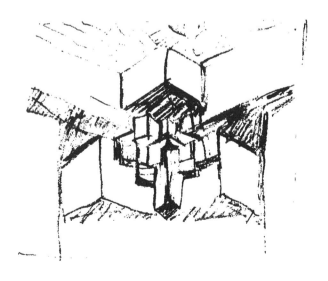

5 Detail of the north façade. The meticulous attention to the
window mullions and the expressive structure of the eaves
add character to the building, while also aligning it with
local architectural tradition.

6 The indentations on the façades, based on organic forms,
contrast with the three-dimensional solidity of the wooden
and stone supports, inspired by rock formations. Jeanneret
made several sketches of crystalline structures and later
reworked them for his architecture.

villa stotzer
villa jaquemet
1908 la chaux-de-fonds

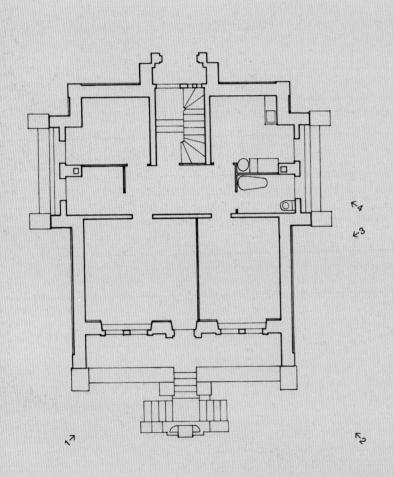

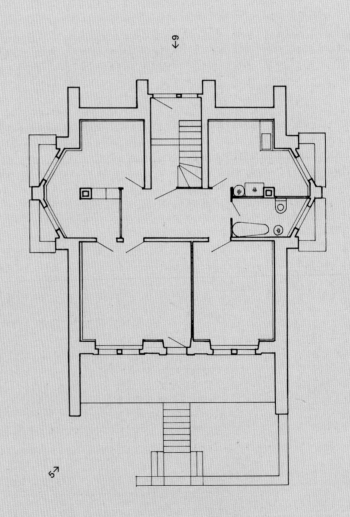

L'Eplattenier, Jeanneret's master, was probably responsible for obtaining the commission for these houses on behalf of his disciple, who at the time was on a study trip to various European cities with his friend and classmate Léon Perrin.

Albert Stotzer, a mechanics professor at the watchmaking school in La Chaux-de-Fonds, and Ulysse-Jules Jaquemet, a watch polisher, were both relatives of Louis Fallet, Jeanneret's first client. The briefs for their houses were similar (while different from Fallet's): from the outside, they should look like family homes, but inside they should contain two separate apartments – one to live in and one to rent out. Both plots were very close to each other (and also to the Villa Fallet), so the characteristics of the terrain were similar, although Jaquemet's was distinguished by its gentler gradient.

These coincidences, along with the fact that Jeanneret drew up the two projects simultaneously during his stay of almost five months in Vienna, resulted in two houses with a basically identical interior organization, while their exterior forms remained faithful to the concept of regionalism and the teachings of L'Eplattenier. As in the case of the Villa Fallet, the technical aspects were handled by the architect René Chapallaz.

The entrances to both houses were set on the highest parts of the plots, to the north, while the principal rooms – lounge, dining room and master bedroom – faced south, to take advantage of the sunshine and better views. The layout of the Villa Fallet was an obvious precedent in this respect, not only for these particular houses but also for Jeanneret's subsequent buildings. The ground floors are prolonged toward the exterior by means of a terrace, which is highlighted in the Villa Stotzer by the side staircases leading to the garden.

Both houses made use of local materials, treated with all the respect advocated by L'Eplattenier and taking into account the harsh climate of the Jura. Solid stone walls emphasize the houses' rustic character and root them in the land (both physically and conceptually), while the roofs are steeply sloped with substantial overhangs, supported by exposed wooden corbels, to provide protection from the snow.

The point where the walls meet the ground is softened in the Villa Jaquemet by the former's slight curve, while the addition of the steps framing the cellar in the Villa Stotzer similarly establishes a more gradual transition. Furthermore, the façades bear witness to a marked hierarchy, with greater significance given to those facing the landscape than the sides and the entrances.

Notwithstanding all the above, and despite the two houses' adherence to L'Eplattenier's vernacular academicism, they represent not only Jeanneret's final expression of that traditionalism – which he began to reassess as a result of his experiences and contacts abroad – but also his first attempts at an incipiently modern architecture. From here on, geometry would play a key role, as both a regulatory element and an expression of an autonomous discipline that would gradually overcome a building's traditional mimetic dependency on its site.

In effect, both houses display a clarity and volumetric autonomy that, rather than seeking organic integration into its context, instead assert the buildings' distinctive qualities, based on the elegance of their proportions and a greater restraint in the ornamental details compared to the Villa Fallet. The ample sections of the structural elements, the emphatic buttresses and mouldings visible on the sides of both houses, the use of concrete slabs between the load-bearing walls and the meticulous geometry governing the sequences of windows all point up Jeanneret's interest in the renewal of architectural language.

This coexistence of nature and artifice, of visual appeal and cerebral form, has been interpreted, metaphorically, as a reflection of Jeanneret's own family background, where his father's manual and physical labour contrasted with his mother's abstract, musical training. Whatever its source, this duality would become an inherent principle of the architect's subsequent work.

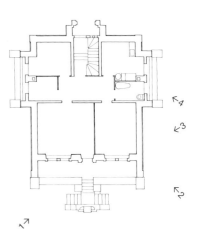

1

2

3

4

1 Opposite: Villa Stotzer. View of the south façade, with windows of the main rooms of the house. The rustic stone ties the house to the locality, while the successive series of steps counteract the gradient and allow the house to be gradually integrated into the terrain. The careful sequential arrangement of the windows signals an evolution towards a form of architecture that is less vernacular and more aware of what will become the guiding principles of modernity.

2 and 3 East façade (opposite) and a detail (above left). In contrast to the Villa Fallet, the façades of the Villa Stotzer have no stucco decoration; this absence, along with the prominent geometrical forms, gives the house a degree of distinctiveness and autonomy.

4 This detail of the east façade reveals the generous proportions of the buttresses, mouldings and other structural elements, as well as Jeanneret's desire to highlight the geometrical nature of these features. All in all, the Villa Stotzer displays the early signs of a reassessment of the historicist idiom.

5 Villa Jaquemet: view of the south façade. As in the case of the Villa Stotzer, the entrance is set on the highest part of the land, on the north side. The two houses are close to each other and were drawn up at the same time. Their interior layout is similar: their living rooms and master bedrooms look out on the south-facing terrace, with splendid views of the landscape. They also share the same exterior forms and materials (still used in accordance with local tradition). The vertical thrust of the stone on the corners of the walls and the gentle rhythm of the windows create a well-judged static equilibrium that is offset by the striking oblique angles of the roof.

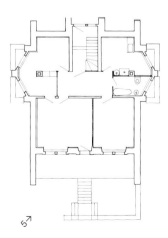

6 North façade. As in the case of the previous buildings, the different façades establish a hierarchy determined by the lay of the land and the need to take full advantage of both the sunlight and the views. The south side therefore takes on greater expressive importance than the north side, which provides the entrance to the house. The design of the Villa Stotzer's north façade differs greatly from Jeanneret's original ideas, as can be seen from his sketches.

villa jeanneret-perret

1912 la chaux-de-fonds

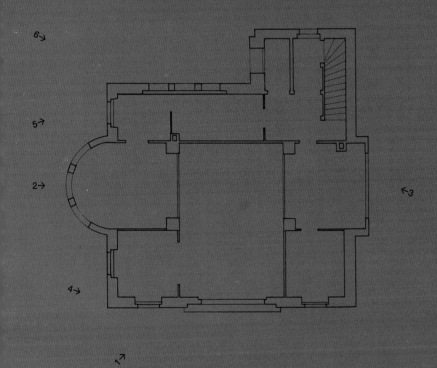

Jeanneret settled in La Chaux-de-Fonds during the Christmas period of 1911, after a long study trip that, apart from a few interruptions, had lasted since September 1907, just after the completion of the Villa Fallet. As soon as he was back, his parents entrusted him with the design of their new house, on the Rue de Montagne, very close to the Villas Fallet, Stotzer and Jaquemet.

The Villa Jeanneret-Perret, however, is strikingly different from these earlier works, as a result of the experience that the young architect had acquired on his travels and the contacts that he had made in the process (in particular, Behrens, Wright and Hoffmann). On his journey to the Near East, it was the mosques and humble wooden houses of Constantinople that had most attracted his attention. Shortly afterwards, during his stay in Greece, he was deeply impressed by the Acropolis (which he visited every day for four weeks) and the design of the Parthenon.

Le Corbusier, drawing of Hagia Sophia in Constantinople

The development of his thinking was also marked by Alexandre Cingria-Vaneyre's book *Les Entretiens de la Ville du Rouet* (Geneva, 1908), which not only advocated the use of geometrical forms but also argued that Swiss architecture was more closely linked to the Mediterranean peoples than the Germanic tradition.

Le Corbusier, drawing of the Propylaea, In the Acropolis in Athens

Although all these factors are present in Jeanneret's new approach, the most obvious influence on this villa is the neoclassicism that was dominant in Germany at that time, particularly that of Peter Behrens, with whom he had worked for five months in 1910 and 1911. Armed with all these references, Jeanneret did not so much make a break with the regionalism espoused by his master L'Eplattenier as uninhibitedly revise it and move it towards classicism.

The white façades of the Villa Jeanneret-Perret contrast sharply with the rustic stonework of his previous work. They herald the gradual renunciation of a vernacular outlook for a classical viewpoint and a transition from a decorative mentality concerned with surface details to a focus on greater spatial richness, achieved by the combination of simple cube-shaped elements.

The building is set on a sloping plot, reached by climbing a path up to the terrace – an architectural promenade derived from Jeanneret's visits to the Parthenon. Once at the platform that serves as the base of the house, visitors must continue around to the rear of the house to come to the entrance.

The walk from the garden entrance to the plinth supporting the building is not linear but, as might be expected, weaves its way upwards. This is partly determined by the steep terrain, but it is also designed to make the approach slower and less direct, thereby establishing a dialogue that integrates the house's geometric simplicity into its lush natural surroundings. The south-facing main façade, with its fine views and optimal reception of sunlight, is seen to particularly good effect on this winding route.

Inside the villa, the ground floor is arranged around four central columns around which the daytime spaces are arranged; the dining area is especially striking, with a semicircular apse that projects out onto the terrace and adds character to the façade.

On the upper floor, the windows are set under the eaves to form a horizontal strip, interrupted by columns decorated with local plant motifs. Apart from the customary domestic spaces, an ample music room was designed for the architect's mother, Marie Jeanneret-Perret, to give her piano lessons, while his father, Georges-Édouard Jeanneret-Gris, was allocated a workshop.

With its pristine white walls, regular geometric form and pergola on the terrace, the Villa Jeanneret-Perret seems closer to the clarity and sunshine of the Mediterranean than the darkness and harsh winters of the Jura mountains.

1

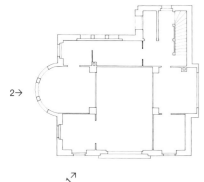

2→

1→

1 The building stands on the highest part of the grounds and is reached via a winding climb that brings it slowly into view. The south face has a strip of windows running along the upper floor, with projecting eaves that provide protection from bad weather. The columns interrupting the windows bear ornamental motifs inspired by the surrounding countryside, as was customary in Jeanneret's early buildings. The wall to the left compensates for the gradient; it has an opening that allows visitors to pass through and continue the architectural promenade.

2 West façade, seen from the terrace. The dining room, in the form of an apse, gives personality to the façade with its expressive, semicircular lines. The overall austerity and the steady sequencing of the openings owe more to classical order than local tradition.

3

4

5

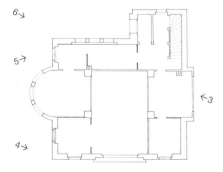

3 Partial view of the east façade. Despite the profuse vegetation, the house stands out with assertive independence. Jeanneret rejected local materials such as stone and eliminated all ornamentation from the walls in favour of pristine whiteness; these factors combine with the geometric simplicity of the forms to give the villa a luminosity that counteracts the harsh climate of La Chaux-de-Fonds.

4 View of the bridge over the opening in the wall, intended not only as another stage of the architectural promenade but also as a subtle transition towards an increasingly intimate space.

5 The walk continues through the arch in the background before finally reaching the entrance to the house. The view of the terrace, on the left, shows the pergola, a feature more typical of warmer climates.

6 Opposite: The pergola is visible in the foreground, prolonging the north façade, where the entrance to the villa is set. The restraint on this side differentiates it from the south façade, which is the real showpiece of the Villa Jeanneret, favoured by its orientation and superb views.

villa schwob

1916 la chaux-de-fonds

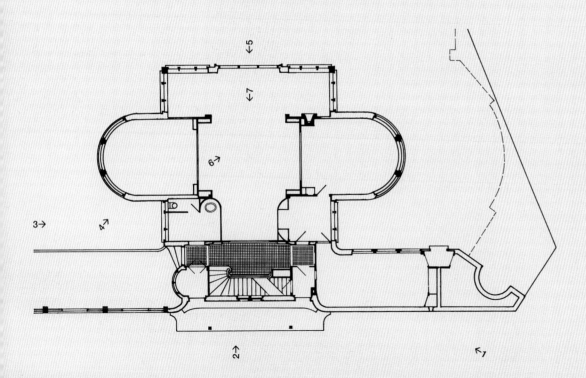

'You knew how to evaluate the definitive achievement of this work that I conceived and oversaw down to the smallest detail and that was as much a necessity as a joy for me. I must say, without any modesty, that I was truly surprised by the architectural dignity of this house, by its power and certainty.' (1)

In this letter that Jeanneret wrote from Paris to Camilla Schwob, the wife of the industrialist Anatole Schwob, on 8 September 1919, he highlighted the interest and relevance of this architectural experiment – the first building that he would recognize as entirely his own work. The construction process, however, had been fraught with difficulties and disagreements.

The Schwobs were a famous watchmaking family from La Chaux-de-Fonds, who owned brands such as Tavannes and Cyma. With their cultivated artistic sensitivity, they had been favourably impressed by the villa that Jeanneret built for his parents in 1912, and as a result, entrusted him with this new project, built between August 1916 and September 1917. It was intended to bear witness to the Schwobs' social eminence, but in an unostentatious way; it also provided Jeanneret with an opportunity to create a work of art with an emotional impact. In addition to these two requirements, Jeanneret was keen to put into practice some of the many ideas he had encountered on his travels.

So, although the Villa Schwob is indebted to his parents' house, it is also true that the later building was a synthesis of external references and marked Jeanneret's first clean break with local tradition. The house was therefore conceived as a discourse dotted with quotations: from Perret (due to some similarities with a project drawn up during Jeanneret's time at Perret's studio and the use of reinforced concrete – although Jeanneret used it in accordance with the Dom-ino system that he had developed in 1914–15, which would play a key part in his subsequent definition of the 'Five Points of a New Architecture'); from Josef Hoffmann (Villa Ast); from the Werkbund; from Frank Lloyd Wright (Thomas P. Hardy House, in Racine), and even from Palladio (Casa Palladio or Casa Cogollo, attributed to Andrea Palladio, in Vicenza, 1559–62). These references are drawn from a wide range of places and periods, endowing the Villa Schwob with a semantic density and a distinctly eclectic

Josef Hoffmann, Villa Ast, Vienna, 1909–11

Frank Lloyd Wright, Thomas P. Hardy House, Racine, Wisconsin, 1905

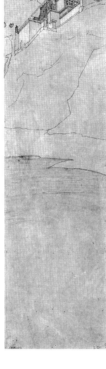

Andrea Palladio, Casa Palladio (Casa Cogollo), Vicenza, 1559–62

personality, with varying degrees of intensity that Jeanneret proved able to control with great skill.

'With architecture as imperious as this, the most important task is to purify, eliminating the superfluous and retaining only what is useful, forceful or serene.' (2)

The plot on which the Villa Schwob was built is situated in a residential area on the eastern edge of the town. The house occupies the highest part of the land and enjoys excellent views of the valley. Reinforced concrete was used for both the structure and the bevelled cornice that crowns the building. The flat roof goes against the Jura tradition of steep gradients to create a purer, more modern form with a terrace on top. The roof's slight slope towards the rear of the house made it possible to install drainpipes inside the house and quickly channel away melted snow before it had a chance to freeze. Hot-air pipes were also set in the walls and gaps in the structure to provide insulation.

The initial plans called for a perfect square, with a double-height living room in the centre and semicircular apses containing the dining room and play room on two opposite sides. The presence of four central columns, marking off the interior space, reflects the influence of the house Jeanneret designed for his parents.

Schwob introduced a number of changes, however: the kitchen, originally set in the basement, ended up next to the wall shutting off the garden, and a closed central space overlooking the street was incorporated, with the stairwell placed behind it. These modifications, along with difficulties in the construction process, partly due to the use of a relatively new material – reinforced concrete – in a small town like La Chaux-de-Fonds, gave rise to misunderstandings and conflicts between the architect and his client:

'You have often reproached me for the reinforced concrete structure. This was the only way of achieving two things: firstly, covering the site before the arrival of winter, because neither the stone quarry nor the brick factory could have supplied the building material for masonry without pillars. Secondly, creating the layout that so enchanted you.' (3)

The many problems associated with the building would eventually play a part in Jeanneret's decision to leave his birthplace, settle in Paris and embark on a new phase of his career, but he nevertheless recognized and staunchly defended the value of this experiment:

'Some problems excite me so much that neither vicissitudes nor disagreements can wrench from me the desire to do everything possible or the joy inherent in this: your villa will be cloaked in the defects and qualities that are intrinsic to me.' (4)

Furthermore, the Villa Schwob already displays a feature that would become a constant in Le Corbusier's later work: duality. This would be expressed through a marked opposition between perceptual exactitude and emotional stimulation, making his architecture an experiment always open to interpretation, a laboratory where influences are crystallized and, more often than not, abstracted from their context and original function to take on new meanings when they are reinterpreted. This is the case here with the contrasting treatment of the façades. The rear, which opens onto the garden, is glazed and brightly lit, while the front, which looks onto the street, is blind and sealed. Despite this difference in approach, derived from the façades' respective positions – enclosure on the colder northern face, openness on the warmer, southern face – their proportions follow the same system of *tracés régulateurs,* or 'regulating lines', as Jeanneret called the set of rules based on the Golden Section.

'The overall mass of the façades, both front and back, is governed by the same angle (A), which determines a diagonal whose multiple parallels and perpendiculars will supply the corrective measurements for the secondary elements, doors, windows, panels, etc., right down to the smallest details.' (5)

Another striking feature of the street façade is the difference in scale between the large blind panel and the four small oval openings, which recall the windows typical of French academic architecture, as well as the contrast between the rotundity of the blind panel and the slender delicacy of the pillars supporting the porch. This façade is rendered even more disconcerting by the ambiguous presence of two apparently identical entrance doors, which open onto the foot of the stairs.

The mysterious, withdrawn nature of this north façade is reminiscent of a harem, earning the house the nickname of the Turkish Villa, in honour of the Byzantine architectural tradition that Jeanneret had studied on his travels. (In Istanbul he photographed a fountain with a blind central panel and small side openings.) This influence can also be seen in the layout of the ground floor, with its side apses characteristic of Byzantine churches, and in the graceful geometry of the cornices on the top of the building, stripped of ornamentation and formally similar to the examples of popular Turkish architecture that Jeanneret would reproduce in his *Voyage d'Orient* (6).

In contrast to the sealed front, the rear is open to sunshine and offers views of the gardens through the large, high windows of the south façade and the double height of the central living room. The ground floor is completed by other rooms (kitchen, office, dining room, play room, library and wardrobe); upstairs, the first floor contains bedrooms and complementary spaces, with more bedrooms and facilities, including a solarium and terrace garden, on the second floor.

The qualitative leap of the Villa Schwob marked a turning point in Jeanneret's career. It features a good many of the elements that would flourish in his later work: the double-height living room, the structural use of reinforced concrete, the adoption of the Dom-ino system, geometry as a regulatory principle, the dynamic alternation of straight and curved lines and the substitution of the traditional sloping roof for a flat one.

All these factors distance the building from local tradition and directly align it with the emerging rationalist architecture. This explains why it is the only work from Le Corbusier's early period that would later appear in his most important written work, specifically in the chapter devoted to regulatory design:

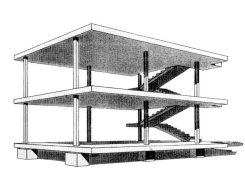

Axonometric of the *Dom-ino* structure

'This small villa stands in the midst of other buildings put up without any rules, as something more monumental and of a different order.' (7)

The Villa Schwob has been restored twice since its completion. The first refurbishment was supervised from 1957 to 1958 by the Milanese architect Angelo Mangiarotti; the second was undertaken in 1987 by the R. and P. Studer architectural studio, based in La Chaux-de-Fonds, and the Parisian interior designer Andrée Putman.

Sources
(1) Claude Garino, with Jean-Bernard Siegfried and the Bureau d'Architecture R. et P. Studer, *Le Corbusier. La Villa Turque, 1916–1917*, La Chaux-de-Fonds, 1987, p. 4 (Letter from Jeanneret-Le Corbusier to Camille Schwob, written from Paris on 8 September 1919)
(2) Claude Garino, *Le Corbusier. La Villa Turque, 1916–1917*, p. 26 (Letter from Jeanneret-Le Corbusier to Camille Schwob, written on 8 September 1919)
(3) Claude Garino, *Le Corbusier. La Villa Turque, 1916–1917*, p. 16 (Letter from Jeanneret-Le Corbusier to Anatole Schwob, written on 24 April 1917)
(4) Claude Garino, *Le Corbusier. La Villa Turque, 1916–1917*, p. 4 (Letter from Jeanneret-Le Corbusier to Anatole Schwob, written from Paris on 24 April 1917)
(5) Le Corbusier, *Vers un architecture*, Paris, 1923
(6) Le Corbusier, *Voyage d'Orient*: *Carnets*, New York, 1988
(7) Le Corbusier, *Vers un architecture*, p. 62

1

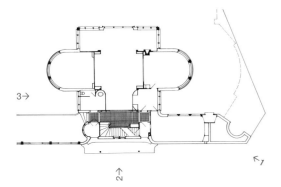

3→

2↑

←1

1   This view from the north-east makes clear the changes
    made in this villa as compared to Jeanneret's previous
    work. The flat roof, in striking contrast to the earlier
    pronounced gradients, evacuates rainwater inside rather
    than outside the building and also serves as a terrace.
    Furthermore, Jeanneret used concrete for the first time in
    both the structure of the house and the exposed, bevelled
    cornice. The initial plans, indebted to the villa Jeanneret
    designed for his parents, basically consisted of a square
    floor plan, with semicircular apses added on two sides.
    This layout was later altered in the course of the
    construction process.

*'This small villa stands in the midst
of other buildings put up without any
rules, as something more monumental
and of a different order.'*

2

3

'The overall mass of the façades,
both front and back, is governed by
the same angle (A), which determines a
diagonal whose multiple parallels and
perpendiculars will supply the corrective
measurements for the secondary
elements, doors, windows, panels, etc.,
right down to the smallest details.'

2   The blind panel on the front of the house masks the stairwell,
    and the uncertainty created by the visual and expressive opacity
    of this north façade is heightened by the placement of two
    identical doors on either side. These extrapolations from
    Byzantine references imbue the house with mystery, and the
    thin, cylindrical columns under the projecting block only serve
    to heighten the visual tension still further.

3   The east façade, with the semicircular space containing a living
    room on the ground floor – the access to the terrace can be
    seen in the photo – and bedroom on the first floor. Here, the
    small openings contrast with the generous proportions of
    those below and echo the similarly discreet oval windows
    on the north side.

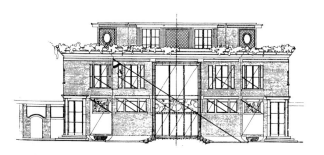

4

5

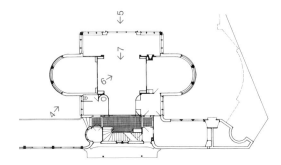

4   Detail of the east façade with the carefully designed brick
    membrane overlaid on the surfaces and mullions, adding
    contrast to the house and setting off its proportions.

5   South façade, overlooking the garden. The duality between
    the respective opacity and transparency of the north and
    south façades is made evident by this double-height space,
    a rectangle that is perfectly proportioned in both its overall
    dimensions and its partitions, emphasizing the geometric
    guidelines applied to the house.

6   View of the large, double-height living room, which opens
    onto the garden from the south façade. The extra height of
    the windows allows light to pour into this space.

7   View of the living room, showing the first-floor corridor that
    provides access to the bedrooms. After an initial restoration
    completed in 1957, the present state of the building is the
    result of a second renovation done thirty years later, with
    the collaboration of the Parisian designer Andrée Putman.

une petite maison

1923–24 vevey

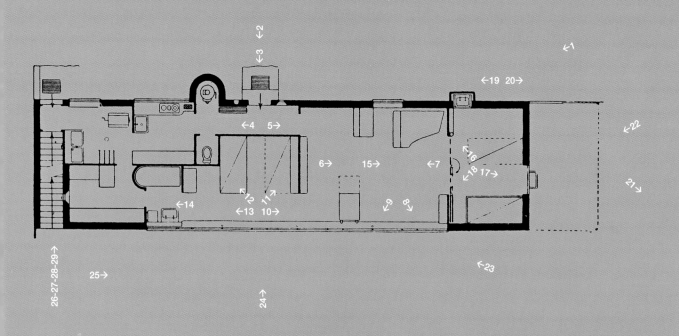

'The problem posed: a house for just two people, with no servants. Region: the eastern end of Lake Geneva; on the shores of the lake, on the dominant slope; front view to the south. The project was undertaken in an unusual way: a precise, functional ground plan was drawn up for the house, corresponding exactly to the programme, an authentic little machine for living in. Then, with the plan completed, we looked for a suitable plot of land.' (1)

The small house in which both Le Corbusier and his brother Albert would spend long periods with their mother – their father died shortly after the building's completion – asserted the autonomy of modern architecture over the impositions of the site. It subverted conventional order and methodology by giving primary importance to the planning stages and placing special emphasis on the key requirements of the programme.

'Was it necessary, in the first place, to look for the land and draw up the plans accordingly? This is the usual method.
I thought that it was better to make an exact ground plan, perfectly in keeping with the intended use, determined by the three factors that I have already mentioned, and, having done this, go out with the plan in my pocket, in search of an advantageous plot of land.
This apparently contradictory procedure points up the key to the problem of modern housing. First deal with the housing, linking together some reasonable functions. Then go and put it in place...' (2)

The programme was developed by means of a sequence of uninterrupted spaces covering the functional requirements, and joined together by the annexes added to each space.

'A machine for living in: each element is assigned a certain number of square metres, with a total of 56 m² for the whole house. These are put together and come to 60 m². In this tiny house, there is a window 11 metres long and the entrance area offers a perspective 14 metres long. The mobile screens and hidden beds make it possible to improvise rooms for guests.' (3)

Le Corbusier, Maison Citrohan, 1920.

This is how Le Corbusier explained the main characteristics of this small family home on the banks of Lake Geneva, based on the model of the Maison Citrohan. Le Corbusier's comments also reveal the double-pronged conceptual focus present in all his work. On the one hand, he proclaimed and defended an international modern architecture that is contextually autonomous and can be mass-produced:

'...the new elements of modern architecture made it possible to find a plot of land in any circumstances.' (4)

On the other hand, Le Corbusier identified with an architecture that was geographically localized (the Mediterranean tradition) and mindful of his personal programme. He described the form of the house – a long, thin, rectangular parallelepiped with a small projection at one end and a large sliding window – as:

'...a constructional innovation formulated to make it possible for a window to become the central player or element of the house.' (5)

This clearly shows the mechanistic focus prevalent in the rationalist thinking of the time.

'Ed has drawn up some very simple plans of a purist house in the form of a wagon...' (6)

The small house, 2.5 m (8 ft) high, fitted the plot

'...like a hand in a glove.' (7)

Situated 4 m (13 ft) from the road and about the same distance from the lake, the house is sheltered by a wall that surrounds it and visually isolates it from the exterior to the north, east and west.

'...the omnipresent and omnipotent landscape on all fronts ends up being tiring... Have you noticed that, in these conditions, "no one looks at it any more"? In order for the landscape to be taken into account, it is necessary to limit it...' (8)

Nevertheless, a window was put into the stone wall on the south façade to frame and highlight a fragment of the impressive landscape formed by the lake and the Alps.

'The south wall, however, was perforated with a square opening to "proportion" it (adapt it to human dimensions) and also to create shade and coolness.' (9)

Le Corbusier set a table supported by a single central leg in the garden, backing onto this opening. The choice of one window to select and emphasize a fragment of the natural landscape reappears in both the Villa Meyer and the Villa Savoye; in the latter case, it serves as the end point of the upward architectural promenade running from the exterior to the interior. The part of the wall that runs parallel to the large 11-m (36 ft) gap drops in height,

'...is suddenly interrupted and the show begins: light, space, this water and these mountains.' (10)

This sets up an all-embracing view of the lake from the interior of the house, thereby fusing the exterior and interior and

'...allowing the grandeur of a magnificent place to enter the house: the lake, with its movement, the Alps, with the miracle of the light.' (11)

Years later, the façade was given added protection from the harsh weather in the form of corrugated aluminium cladding, of the type used in the construction of the fuselage of planes. It hardly need be pointed out that this modification was entirely to the liking of Le Corbusier, as it emphasized the metaphor of the house as a machine.

'This utilitarian shell is forcefully beautiful... In this way, the small house was brought up to date (without any preconceived intention).' (12)

The interior layout, for its part, creates an architectural promenade around the perimeter of the house that ends up in the garden-room:

'...a lounge with greenery, an interior.' (13)

The dividing partitions in the main rooms – the mother's bedroom and the living room – are cut off before reaching the southern enclosing wall, thus maintaining the continuity of the large window and the ledge running along its length, as well as making it easier to adjust the position of the table and swivelling lamp according to the sunlight.

Le Corbusier, bathroom in the Villa Savoye, Poissy, 1929–31

The transition between the living room and the garden is marked by a versatile space used as a guest bedroom, with a washbasin and cupboard hidden behind three sliding screens. The washbasin sets up a protuberance on the north façade, underlying Le Corbusier's desire to give prominence to secondary elements; such features reappear elsewhere, as in the placement of the bathtub behind a partition, both here and in the Villa Savoye, and in the protruding confessionals in Notre Dame-du-Haut. In the Petite Maison, these dual spaces emphasize the building's machine-like quality.

Le Corbusier, interior and exterior projection of the confessionals at the chapel of Notre-Dame-du-Haut, Ronchamp, 1954

Both the bathroom and the small bedroom on the top floor receive natural light through small, high windows, whose size and soft light seem further reduced by the dark paint on the walls. This effect contrasts with the bright exterior and 11-m (36-ft) stretch of window, which is the real star of the Petite Maison. This use of light to define space is a basic feature of Le Corbusier's work and recurs throughout his career. One of many examples is the striking differentiation between the shadowy communal spaces – the internal streets – of the Unité in Marseilles, and the bright clarity that fills the private spaces – the apartments.

Sources
(1) Le Corbusier, *The Complete Architectural Works, vol. 1, 1910–1929,* London, 1964, p. 74
(2) Le Corbusier, *Précisions sur un état présent de l'architecture et de l'urbanisme,* Paris, 1960
(3) Le Corbusier, *The Complete Architectural Works, vol. 1, 1910–1929,* p. 74
(4) Le Corbusier, *Précisions sur un état présent de l'architecture et de l'urbanisme,* p. 149
(5) Le Corbusier, *Une petite maison,* Basel, 2001, p. 30
(6) Georges-Édouard Jeanneret, 'Journal', 27 December 1923 (Quoted in Bruno Reichlin, 'La petite maison à Corseaux. Une analyse structurale', in *Le Corbusier à Genève 1922–1932,* exhibition catalogue, Geneva, 1987, p. 10)
(7) Le Corbusier, *Une petite maison,* p. 9
(8) Le Corbusier, *Une petite maison,* pp. 22–23
(9) Le Corbusier, *Une petite maison,* p. 26
(10) Le Corbusier, *Une petite maison,* p. 27
(11) Le Corbusier, *Précisions sur un état présent de l'architecture et de l'urbanisme,* p. 152
(12) Le Corbusier, *Une petite maison,* p. 21
(13) Le Corbusier, *Une petite maison,* p. 24

'Henceforth, the fury of vehicles will replace the silence of Arcadia. Luckily, the face of the Petite Maison is on the other side, protected.'

1 and 2 General and partial views of the north façade as seen from the road, on which the building turns its back with an essentially closed façade, in contrast with the south façade, which has a large horizontal opening overlooking the lake. The wall, which runs along the length of the grounds, visually separates the house from the street, emphasizing the desire for privacy.

3

4

5

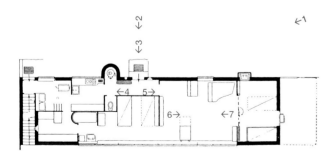

3 Main entrance to the house. Note the cladding of corrugated aluminium sheets, which protects the façade from bad weather.

4 Once the threshold is crossed, a right turn leads directly to the kitchen and larder.

5 A left turn, however, leads to the living room. A small unit contains a radiator, while also blocking the view into the interior.

6

7

6 The interior space takes the form of a flowing sequence of functions: the living room, the multifunctional space and, finally, the garden. The intentional shadiness of the multipurpose area is achieved by filtering sunshine through the high window set next to the ceiling and further increased by the dark colour of the walls. This effect contrasts with the uninhibited brightness on either side, from the living room and the garden.

7 This view from the flexible, multifunctional space clearly shows the long window that stretches uninterrupted towards the bedroom of Jeanneret's mother, which is separated from the living room by a partition that stops before it reaches the outer wall.

8

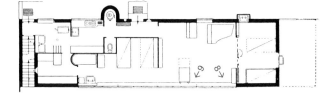

8 This window opening, 11 metres (36 ft) long, provides an
   extraordinary view of Lake Geneva, converting the south
   façade into a breathtaking canvas that changes according
   to the time of day or season of the year.

9 Opposite: The swivelling lamp and table can be moved to
   adapt to changes in the direction of the sunlight.

9

'A single window eleven metres long unifies and clarifies all these elements, allowing the grandeur of a magnificent setting to enter into the house: the lake, with its movement, and the Alps, with the miracle of the light.'

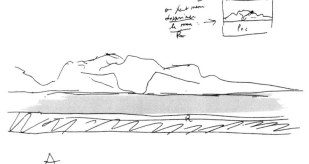

10

11

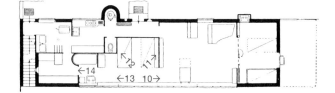

10 View of the bedroom showing the entire extension of the window and the ledge that reinforces its horizontality. The partition separates this space from the living room, although they are unified by the wide gap.

11 Detail of the bedroom, personalized by the salmon pink of its walls and a desk designed by the architect himself.

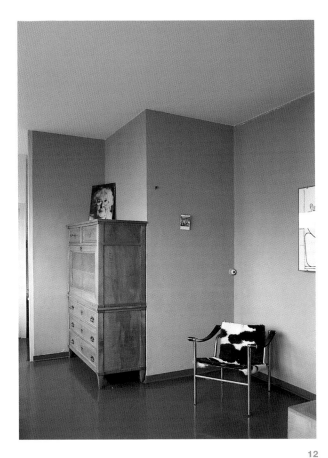

12
13
14

12, 13 and 14 Bedroom details. The series of short folds in the
partitions jut out towards the window, the room's fourth vertical
enclosing element. The space is unified by the unbroken
colouring of the walls, setting off their jagged lines against the
smooth surface of the south façade. The sink, set alongside
the window ledge, and the bathtub, tucked behind a partition,
frame the wardrobe door.

15

16

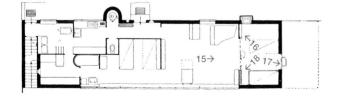

15 and 16 The wooden panel used to separate the living room from the dining room when the latter is serving as a bedroom. The sink built into the wall forms a protuberance that can be seen outside, on the north façade.

17 and 18 Opposite: The versatility of the living room is rounded off by the incorporation of a bed alongside the door to the garden and a cupboard hidden behind the sliding screen door.

17

18

*'The mobile screens and hidden beds make it possible
to improvise rooms for visitors.'*

19

20

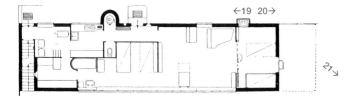

19 North façade, separated from the boundary wall by a strip of land 4 metres (13 ft) wide. In the foreground, the protuberance formed by the washbasin inside.

20 The house is prolonged by a small overhang that is closed off on one side by a screen. The passageway leads to the small garden.

21 Opposite: The opening in the wall frames the lake and the Alps, emphasizing their beauty. The wall also works with the large foxglove tree to shelter this area from the sunshine.

'The south wall, however, was perforated with a square opening to "proportion"
it (adapt it to human dimensions) and also to create shade and coolness.'

'Here, the house has four metres (13 ft) of façade. The door on to the garden, three steps, under cover.'

23

24

25

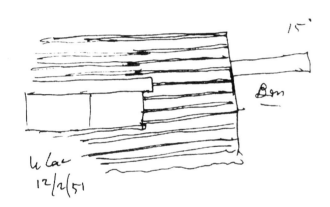

'Cockpits made of corrugated aluminium marked the birth of civil aviation (Breguet). In this way, the small house was brought up to date (without any preconceived intention).'

22 Opposite: The overhang shelters the entrance to the living and dining room from bad weather, as well as providing a space on top that can be used for relaxation.

23 and 24 The 11-m window – the first of many such long windows in the architect's work – is the most representative statement in this little house. The corrugated aluminium sheets placed over the original stucco emphasize both the horizontality of the opening and the concept of the house as a machine.

25 The boundary wall separating the house from the lake runs in parallel to the window. The wall's rusticity contrasts with the building's industrial appearance, and its low height enables the sunshine and views to be enjoyed from inside the house.

26

27

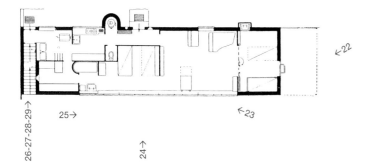

26 and 27 Small bedroom on the upper floor, usually used by Jeanneret himself and his brother. The room had to accommodate the stairwell, so the only way to fit two beds was as bunks.

28 and 29 Opposite: A small writing table raised to receive the light entering through the window under the ceiling. It offers a view of the flat roof, laid with some six inches of soil to grow a variety of grasses. In the background, Lake Geneva and the Alps.

'The roof garden survives
autonomously, in tune with the sun,
the rain, the winds and the birds
that carry seeds.'

villa savoye

1929–31 poissy

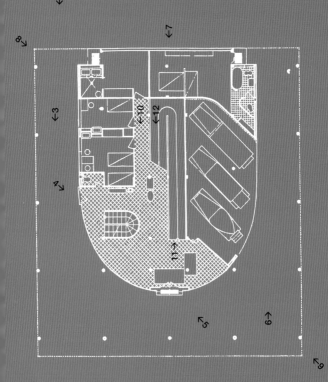
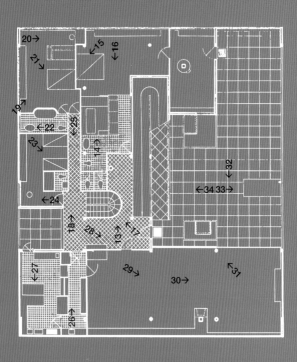
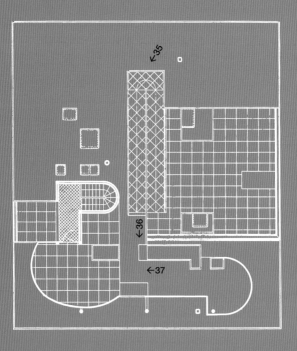

The timelessness that Le Corbusier used to define his clients' aesthetic criteria is undoubtedly the most striking characteristic of the Villa Savoye. It is the paradigm of the machine age – it contains the 'Five Points of a New Architecture': the *pilotis*, the *façade libre*, the *fenêtre en longueur*, the *plan libre* and the *toit-jardin* – while also drawing on the essential values of classical architecture.

As a modern artefact, the Villa Savoye relates to its setting with total formal autonomy: it can be seen as pure, pristine geometry, a *Gestalt* that confronts the curved lines of nature with abstract orthogonality, without any attempt to blend into its surroundings.

The house was placed in the centre of the plot, a high observatory unified by the horizontal windows running along the façades, like a container with views of the exterior. Three of the house's four façades were cut off to reveal the slender pilotis, heightening the impression of an elevated plane, of a vantage point. At the same time, the building's placement in the middle of the grounds sets it apart as a pure, eye-catching form.

This visual duality between the house as a vantage point and its centripetal spatial organization, turned in on itself, can be seen in the importance given to these two aspects in the first-floor terrace, both in its alignment with the sun and the provision of extensive views of the exterior.

Despite Le Corbusier's vision of an isolated residence, he defined the house as an *objet-type*, a model that could be built in series; he would later propose to do just that in his plans for the Buenos Aires neighbourhood of Le Vingtième, made up of twenty copies of the Villa Savoye.

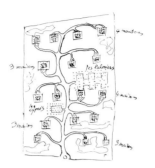

Le Corbusier, adaptation of the Villa Savoye for mass construction in the Le Vingtième neighbourhood, Buenos Aires

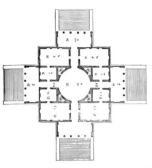

Andrea Palladio, floor plan of the Villa Rotonda, Vicenza, *c.* 1550

This description of the beauty of the landscape, with its allusion to the ideals of Virgil's *Georgics* – a key reference in Le Corbusier's *Précisions sur un état présent de l'architecture et de l'urbanisme* – echoes Palladio's description of his Villa Capra-Rotonda (Vicenza, *c.* 1550):

This similarity enabled Colin Rowe to link the two buildings and affirm the classical, timeless nature of the Villa Savoye:

The shared characteristics of both buildings include placement on a plinth – to isolate the villa and make it stand out from its surroundings – and the reversibility and treatment of the façades.

Moreover, both buildings are stratified in three clearly identifiable parts, suggesting the metaphor of base/shaft/capital. These shared features define the two villas' essentialist nature and monumental timelessness.

As it happens, the Villa Savoye was barely used by its owners and is now a monument open to visitors, with a meticulously compiled colour scheme that enhances its expressiveness. It has been painstakingly reconstructed after a series of misadventures (it was used as a barn by the Nazis and subsequently suffered a long period of abandonment and deterioration).

The house is made up of three differentiated masses: the ground floor, which contains the communal service areas, a small guest apartment and the garage; the house proper on the first floor, with the dining room, kitchen, bedrooms, bathrooms and a terrace; and finally, the roof garden, which serves as a second terrace and solarium. All these spaces are linked by the purifying journey of the *promenade architecturale*.

The journey begins with the main access road for cars, which rises up towards the site; visitors must then turn onto a side road to reach the house, which slowly comes into view through the trees. This route – not frontal and direct but side-on and almost accidental – also means that the house must be circled before the entrance at the rear is reached; it also illustrates one of the guiding principles of the rationalist concept: the space–time dimension in modern architecture, although Le Corbusier draws on other cultural references as well.

Approaching cars thus come right to the main door, on the southern façade, as part of the ritual of mechanical integration of the vehicle and the building: 'the house is a machine for living in'. The taut glass membrane enclosing the ground floor echoes the turning circle of a car; its dynamic curvature defines the function of the space within (movement, circulation), and its transparency reveals its public nature.

El Lissitzky, *Prounenraum*, Berlin, 1923

'So, the door to the house is reached by car, and the arc of the minimum turning circle of a car provides the dimensions of the house. The car enters under the pilotis, turns around the communal services, arrives at the centre, at the door to the hall, goes into the garage or continues on its way back: this is the basic theme.' (8)

In contrast with the lightness and visual dynamism of the ground floor, the *piano nobile* becomes a static, floating slab with streamlined rectilinear forms, which rests gently on the ground by means of pilotis, a dotted line that indicates the motion of the car. The opposition of the two planes, one of the dualities that are constantly present in the Villa Savoye, is emphasized by the square floor plan, corresponding to a grid of 5 x 5 pilotis, which, however, becomes a rectangular space on the first floor, due to the slight prolongation of two of its façades.

Following the same criteria, the exterior reticular order of the pilotis is unexpectedly altered inside, adapting to the partitions and giving priority to the comings and goings of the house's inhabitants. So, the piloti that would, in theory, block the entrance once the threshold is crossed, in fact divides into two to frame the sides of the doorway.

The ground floor sees the foundation of two elements that link the different planes: the staircase and the ramp. The spiral staircase drills through the building vertically, contrasting with the house's predominant openness and horizontality. It twists around on itself in an egocentric fashion, returning obsessively to the same point. Beside it, the ramp becomes a communication element integrated into the space, forming its backbone and triggering a series of perceptual experiences, an architectural promenade through a space–time continuum that Le Corbusier borrowed from the traditional architecture of North Africa (*l'espace arabe*).

'Arab architecture provides us with a valuable lesson. It is appreciated on the move, on foot; by walking and moving around, one can see how the architecture's ordering devices unfurl. This principle is opposed to baroque architecture, which is conceived on paper, around a fixed theoretical point. I prefer the teachings of Arab architecture.' (9)

The ramp ends on the first floor, opposite the living and dining room, a space with walls that open up gradually, moving from opacity to total transparency by fusing with the exterior terrace. The latter constitutes an open-air 'room' that is partially closed and makes for a splendid observatory.

'Standing on the grass, one cannot see very far. What is more, grass is unhealthy, damp, etc…to live on; as a result, the house's real garden will not be on the ground, but three and a half metres above the ground: this will be the hanging garden, whose ground is dry and healthy, and it is from there that the landscape can be properly seen, much better than from below.' (10)

In order to integrate the house with the exterior, Le Corbusier used both the *fenêtre en longueur*, interrupted only by woodwork, and the horizontal plane of the window ledge, which, apart from its various practical uses, emphasizes the house's horizontality. Similar methods of spatial integration can be observed in other parts of the villa. In the bedrooms, for example, the brickwork furniture divides and delimits the space but also unifies it, while at the same time satisfying specific requirements with its calculated formal ambiguity. In this field, Adolf Loos had already championed brickwork furniture incorporated into the architecture as a clear example of a modern approach to the planning of space:

Adolf Loos, dressing room, Müller House, Prague, 1930

'The walls of a house belong to the architect. He can do what he wants with them; and this is also true of furniture that is not mobile. It must not look like furniture. It is part of the wall and has no life of its own, unlike those extravagant cupboards that are not modern.' (11)

The Villa Savoye makes extensive use of this device, and the built-in wall-cupboards and work surfaces in the kitchen are a magnificent example of both functional flexibility and spatial integration.

'But the promenade continues. From the upper garden, one goes up the ramp to the roof of the house, where the solarium is.' (12)

The solarium, the ultimate expression of the healthy, open-air life, is protected by a wall in the form of a screen that embodies all the house's metaphorical richness and its continuous interplay of dualities. Its curving, concave and convex forms alternate with taut, linear planes, and it can be understood as a volume or a thin membrane, according to the vantage point. An opening in the screen, opposite the ramp, frames a fragment of landscape and heralds the end of the architectural promenade – a journey in which geometry is a means but not an end; a system that avoids chaos and arbitrariness, as well as rigid mathematical conformity, by means of attractive scene-setting; an emotional challenge set in the context of a controlled higher order.

'In this house, there is a true architectural promenade, offering constantly changing, unexpected and sometimes surprising views. It is interesting to achieve such diversity when there is, for example, from a constructional point of view an utterly strict pattern of pillars and beams.' (13)

Moreover, the sculptural treatment of the screen contrasts with the rigid orthogonality of the *piano nobile* in the same way as the glass membrane on the ground floor. This makes it possible to see the house as a set of meticulously defined proportions, with a perfect hierarchical control of its components and a harmonious integration of the individual parts and the whole – all essential attributes of classical architecture.

'So far, visitors have looked around the interior again and again, asking what is going on, finding it very hard to understand the reasons for what they see and feel; they cannot find anything of what they would call a "house". They feel as if they are inside something completely new.' (14)

In effect, the unusual syntax of the Villa Savoye makes it seem like an abstract form, impeding any direct identification with the usual conventions and instead demanding a renewal of the codes for living. Through this extraordinary architectural discourse, Le Corbusier took the building beyond the context of its time and place. Once its initial function as a paradigm of modernity had run its course, the Villa Savoye took its rightful place as a universal classic.

Sources
(1) Le Corbusier, *The Complete Architectural Works, vol. 2, 1929–1934*, London, 1964, p. 24
(2) Le Corbusier, *The Complete Architectural Works, vol. 2, 1929–1934*, p. 24
(3) Le Corbusier, *The Complete Architectural Works, vol. 1, 1910–1929*, London, 1964, p. 187
(4) Le Corbusier, *Précisions sur un état présent de l'architecture et de l'urbanisme*, Paris, 1960
(5) Andrea Palladio, *Quattro libri dell'Architettura* (quoted in Manfred Wundram and Thomas Pape, *Andrea Palladio*, Munich, 1990, p. 186)
(6) Colin Rowe, *The Mathematics of the Ideal Villa and Other Essays*, Cambridge, Mass., 1976, p. 3
(7) Le Corbusier, *The Complete Architectural Works, vol. 1, 1910–1929*, p. 186
(8) Le Corbusier, *The Complete Architectural Works, vol. 2, 1929–1934*, p. 24
(9) Le Corbusier, *The Complete Architectural Works, vol. 2, 1929–1934*, p. 24
(10) Le Corbusier, *The Complete Architectural Works, vol. 2, 1929–1934*, p. 24
(11) Adolf Loos, 'Ornament und Verbrechen', *Cahiers d'aujourd'hui*, 1913
(12) Le Corbusier, *The Complete Architectural Works, vol. 2, 1929–1934*, p. 24
(13) Le Corbusier, *The Complete Architectural Works, vol. 2, 1929–1934*, p. 24
(14) Le Corbusier, *Précisions sur un état présent de l'architecture et de l'urbanisme*, p. 156

1

2

1→   ↓2

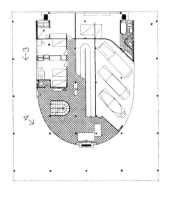

1 and 2 The architectural promenade starts immediately after passing through the boundary wall on the main road. This does not lead directly to the house, however; a side turning has to be taken and the building gradually comes into view as it is approached.

3 and 4 Opposite: The encounter with the house is not frontal but side-on: the ground floor is tucked in to allow a car to pass between it and the pilotis, around the taut glass screen that leads to the main entrance on the south façade.

3

4

'The simple pillars on the ground floor, with their precise layout, cut up the landscape with a regularity that has the effect of suppressing all notions of "front" or "back" of the house, of "side" of the house.'

5

6

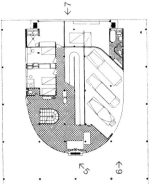

5   Main entrance. The entrance is punctuated by a central pillar and pinpointed by a beam, suggesting the possibility of continuing the journey inside, on foot.

6   Alternatively, the garage door comes into view once the glass plane comes to an end. Finally, as an echo of the approach road on the west façade, the east face indicates the exit route.

7 North façade. The ground floor contains not only the garage but also the communal services and a small apartment for the temporary use of visitors. This floor's limited dimensions allow a car to pass under the house itself, following the perimeter of the building to reach the entrance on the opposite side, thereby achieving the desired mechanistic integration of vehicle and house.

8

9

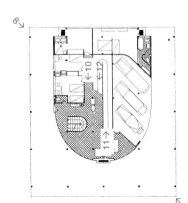

8 and 9 North-east and south-east views. The building seems to be weightless, raised on pilotis that make it independent from the land. The undifferentiated treatment of the two façades, devoid of all hierarchical symbolism, combines with the strip of windows running along the perimeter of the first floor and the placement in the midst of open land to bring to mind the image of an observatory.

'The house is a box in the air, pierced all round, without interruption, by a horizontal window.'

10

11

10 This view from the interior unit of the garage shows the two elements of vertical communication: the ramp and the staircase. The sink in the centre might suggest the ablutions undertaken before taking part in a ritual: perhaps the walk through the building itself.

11 The ramp, a basic element of interior communication, drills its way upwards and provides a dynamic contrast to the house's predominant horizontality.

'...one rises imperceptibly by means of a ramp, which is a completely different sensation from going up a flight of stairs. A staircase separates one floor from another; a ramp connects.'

12 As the ramp rises, the walls are cut away to reveal both the distance that has been covered and the route ahead, thus creating a vibrant interrelationship between fluid spaces.

13 The point where the ramp reaches the first floor, where the house proper begins, does not mark the end of the walk: the glass wall of the terrace shows how it may be continued up the slope. In the background, the entrance to the master bedroom.

14

14 Part of the master bedroom, seen from the bathroom. The white tiles on the surrounding surfaces and the contoured bench, made of brick and topped with mosaic tiles, underline the importance of hygiene and, along with the open terrace, extol the virtues of healthy living.

15

16

15 and 16 General views of the bedroom area. The merging of the bedroom and bathroom spaces, barely separated by a curtain, is a fruit of the quest for spatial integration. Brickwork elements serve as visual filters, as well as containers, but they do not reach the ceiling in order to maintain spatial integration. A skylight allows sunshine to enter the bathroom space, thereby compensating for its distance from the windows on the façade.

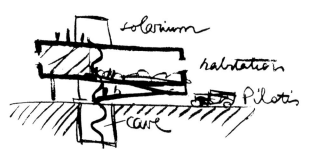

'This spiral staircase, a pure vertical organ, is freely inserted into the horizontal composition.'

17

17 Opposite: The spiral staircase is, along with the ramp, the element that most effectively counteracts the overall horizontality; it sets up a particularly strong counterpoint with the floor tiles on the first storey. Its enclosed, inward-turning curves also contrast with the ramp's open form.

18 Corridor with entrances to the various bedrooms. At the far end, the bedroom allocated to the owners' son.

19 In the above-mentioned bedroom, a brickwork unit partially separates the sleeping area from the study space. This unit serves different functions on different sides (wardrobe and work surfaces) and so acquires a formal non-specificity that enables it to become an integral part of the architecture.

20

21

22

20 Study space, near the window and separated from the sleeping area by the brickwork unit on the right.

21 General view of the bedroom, showing the door as seen from the study space. The curved partition, the result of the bathtub protruding from the other side, personalizes this space and places the emphasis on a secondary element – a technique that Le Corbusier would use in many future buildings.

22 General view of the bathroom adjacent to the bedroom, showing how the bathtub fits into the space created by the partition.

23 Bedroom usually reserved for guests. Once again, a brickwork volume serves not only as a cupboard but also as a visual obstacle that gives privacy to the sleeping area.

24 Partial view of the bedroom. The window, situated in one corner, frames a fragment of the landscape, which is emphasized by the austerity of the walls around it. The vivid colour of one of them marks one edge of the window, as well as providing a canvas for the rich variations in natural light that create the room's poetic intensity.

25

25 View down the corridor to the kitchen. The narrowness of this passageway is visually intensified by the darkness of the right-hand wall. The sunshine filtering through the skylight gradually washes out the bright blue of the wall, with variations over the course of the day.

26 Partial view of the entrance to the kitchen. On the right, storage shelves; on the left, a partition that marks the transition to the preparation area and which is multifunctional on both sides (partition, storage and work surfaces). Food and utensils can be passed from one side to the other through the opening.

27 On the other side of the partition, the kitchen proper is distinguished by a horizontal plane running around the perimeter that holds the various functional elements. As in the rest of the house, the all-pervading presence of the landscape framed by the window becomes an integral part of the interior composition.

'The kitchen is not exactly the sanctuary of the house, but it is certainly one of the most important places. Both the kitchen and living room are spaces for living in.'

28

29

28 On the left, the door to the first-floor terrace; on the right, the entrance to the living room.

29 General view of the living room, as seen from the entrance. The walls enclosing this space become increasingly transparent as they approach the terrace, until the two spaces are finally separated by two large panes of glass. As elsewhere in the house, the ledge accentuates the dominant horizontality and serves different purposes as it advances (cupboards, mantelpiece, housing for a radiator). The lighting is also integrated into the architecture, as it is fitted into a beam.

30

31

30 The proximity of the sliding window on one side and the transparent dividing wall on the other makes the living room appear to blend with the terrace.

31 The living room is prolonged out onto the open terrace by means of the glass dividing wall; even the section of the mouldings is reduced to the minimum to enhance the effect of integration. At certain times of the day, the sun also helps to minimize the separation between the two spaces. The covered terrace can be seen in the background, on the right.

'Taking their view and their light from the regular outline of the box, the different rooms come together, radiating out from a hanging garden that seems to radiate light and sun.'

32 General view, as seen from the covered terrace. The space is prolonged on this plane into the living room and, on the top level, by the solarium, bounded by a curved wall.

33 and 34 As in other buildings designed by Le Corbusier, the series of dualities in the Villa Savoye prevent it from being viewed complacently, without any jolts, and demand instead an active, multi-faceted intellectual approach. So, one wall on the terrace emphasizes the house's persistent and predominant horizontality by incorporating a table, a generously sized plane running perpendicular to the façade. This apparent stillness is disrupted by a 180-degree turn on the other side of the terrace that shows off the dynamic obliqueness of the ramp as it slopes up towards the solarium.

35 The architectural promenade continues from the terrace to the solarium on the roof; this space enjoys the benefits of open air, contact with nature and isolation from the noise of activities on the lower floors.

36

37

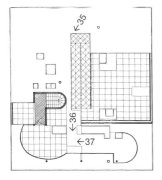

36 The walk ends with an opening in the wall that frames a fragment of the landscape, highlighted by the end of the railings on the left, and the flower bed on the right. The screen wall perforated by this opening serves no structural function but instead acts as a membrane blocking the view and providing protection from the wind.

37 Furthermore, the screen's dynamic web of curves, straight lines and concave planes contrasts with the static appearance of the paving stones and fits snugly into the space, softening the aggressive impact of the sharp edges on the smooth, continuous planes.

pavillon suisse

1930–32 paris

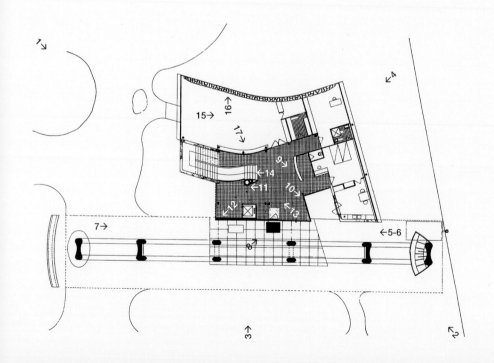

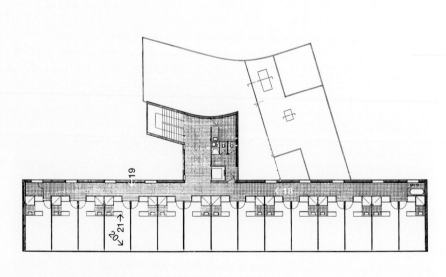

Le Corbusier and his cousin Pierre Jeanneret originally rejected the commission to design the Pavillon Suisse, but they eventually agreed to build it, on a tight budget, at one end of the Cité Universitaire in Paris. The project was greeted with suspicion and contempt by the more conservative sectors of Swiss society, but expert opinion recognized it as one of Le Corbusier's most significant works and it exerted a powerful influence on post-war architecture.

In fact, this commission from the Comité des Universités Suisses (without a preceding competition) can be seen as a gesture to make amends for the last-minute loss of the project to build the headquarters of the League of Nations in 1927, which had virtually been promised to Le Corbusier. It was this disappointment that caused the architects to turn down the later offer, but the insistence of the Comité and the interventions of, among others, the architect Karl Moser, the critic Sigfried Giedion and Professor Fueter, from the mathematics faculty at Zurich University, convinced them to take on this project for a students' hall of residence.

The building was put up in south Paris, at one end of the grounds of the Cité Universitaire, created in 1921 to accommodate foreign students. Its location, surrounded by greenery, allowed the Pavillon Suisse to use the metaphor of a ship floating on a sea, in this case a sea of green. This impression is reinforced by the placement of the bedroom section on sturdy pilotis, which would reappear with equal bravura years later in Marseilles.

The location provided fine, uninterrupted views to the south – which would later be occupied by sports fields – but an orientation in this direction would have ignored the building's natural access route. As a result, the Pavillon was designed with two façades of similar importance, but each was approached with different conceptual and formal criteria. This expressive autonomy of the façades was the result of a reassessment by Le Corbusier. He had initially designed a continuous, uniform skin that wrapped the building with no indication of the different functions within, but he went on to separate and indicate these functions by means of personalized volumes.

Therefore, for example, the regular forms of the residential section, supported by thick pilotis, contrast with the irregular, curved shapes of the stairwell and other communal facilities, while volumes with different functions are clearly distinguished, but without endangering the overall sense of unity. In this way, Le Corbusier made innovations in building practice by, paradoxically, going back to the origins of architecture.

'From the past, it inherits one of the great ideas of the academic tradition, even though it was never made obvious there: this was the conception of a building as an assembly of volumes, each serving a specified function. The idea is as old as architecture, but Le Corbusier here made it eloquent and comprehensible by thinking not of a building, but of separate functional volumes....' (1)

This use of division is also found elsewhere in Le Corbusier's work, such as in the above-mentioned project for the headquarters of the League of Nations, the Centrosoyuz and the Cité de Refuge, where the spatial sequence of the various areas is specifically spelt out. Later on, Le Corbusier would scatter distinct, autonomous elements around the square of La Tourette – the oratory, crypt, organ, walkway – and on the roof of the Unité in Marseilles – the lift shaft, open-air stage, and gym. In all these cases, he achieved an emotional impact similar to that of the volumes that make up the Pavillon Suisse.

Moreover, the functional separation derived from the choice of a stone wall in the library and a staircase rising behind it to lead to the residential section served to reconcile the awkward conjunction of the rectilinear form that was initially planned with the diagonal of the approach route to the Pavillon. The dialogue between the curve of the wall and the circle of the roundabout seals the union between the two elements; this device had already been used in the Villa Favre-Jacot, one of Le Corbusier's buildings in La Chaux-de-Fonds.

It must not be forgotten, however, that Le Corbusier believed that the logic underpinning any architectural solution should be coupled with a sensitivity that provides equilibrium. As in so many cases, the sequence of contrasting elements had already been tried out in the theoretical space that was

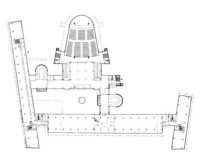

Le Corbusier, ground plan of the third floor of the Centrosoyuz, Moscow, 1929

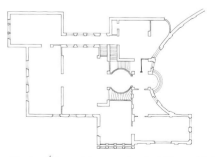

Charles-Édouard Jeanneret, ground floor of the Villa Favre-Jacot, Le Locle, 1912

Le Corbusier's extensive pictorial output, as he himself repeatedly admitted. As William Curtis astutely observes:

'The contrast between oblong flanges and wavy curves was fundamental to Cubist imagery (e.g. guitars), and in the architect's hieroglyphic system these shapes had taken on multiple new associations to do with the contrast between machine and nature, stable geometry and movement, primary functions and circulation, private areas and communal spaces, the assertions of an ideal type and its accommodation of pressures in the setting.' (2)

The section containing the student's bedrooms is, unlike the north face, a clean-cut steel and glass volume whose organic, concrete pilotis detach it from the ground. This effect had already been created in the Villa Savoye, but the latter's streamlined, reticular geometry is far removed from the emphatic forms, materials and dimensions on show in the Pavillon Suisse. The two buildings also share a striking stretch of window, only in this case it forms part of the continuous glass screen on the Pavillon's south façade.

Both these elements provoked fierce criticism from various officials and academic experts, who claimed, not without some foundation, that the pilotis posed structural problems and were vulnerable to wind, and that the glass casing could not guarantee the building's thermal insulation. In effect, as in the case of the Cité de Refuge, Le Corbusier was obliged to add *brises-soleil*. These were confined to the south façade, however, as this was most exposed to sunlight, while the northern wall was covered with sheets of natural stone and only interrupted by small openings. As for the pilotis, their eventual form – a 'dog-bone', in Le Corbusier's own words – was not only visually expressive but also satisfied the requirements of circulation and the drainage system. Moreover, their position in the centre of the building left ample free space around the perimeter, which Le Corbusier repeatedly claimed was not just an area for pedestrian transit but also potentially an outdoor but sheltered lounge area, ideal for chatting and intellectual debate.

'People with no imagination often ask the question "What are these pilotis actually for?"
At a party at Zurich University in 1933, Professor Maurin, the French head of the science faculty, said to Le Corbusier: "I have seen the Pavillon Suisse in the Cité Universitaire. Don't you think that the pilotis that you have used may provide the definitive solution to the increase in traffic in a large town?" Maurin, a physicist who usually worked in a laboratory, spontaneously discovered the rudiments of an architectural and city-planning doctrine that Le Corbusier had been tirelessly propounding for ten years in all his projects and writings.' (3)

Be that as it may, the Pavillon embraced the 'Five Points for a New Architecture' that the Villa Savoye had exalted just two years previously, but they were now freed from restrictive building regulations and enriched by the introduction of new materials and elements. The Pavillon, like the Villa Savoye, is a faithful reflection of the rationalism predominant in the inter-war period, with Le Corbusier as one of its leading lights and staunchest defenders. In this context, the strong desire to liberate the building from the ground by raising it up, along with the glass screen on the south face, corroborates the idea of progress associated with a mechanistic aesthetic.

The fact that the gap between the available technology and the formal proposal made the corresponding technical solution difficult or even unviable did nothing to undermine Le Corbusier's firm convictions, especially in a building of this kind – despite the particularly extreme conditions in which it was built, both physically and economically. It must be borne in mind that the Pavillon Suisse was built on the site of a former quarry, so the foundations had to be strengthened by extending the piles to a depth of up to 19.5 metres (64 feet). In addition, reductions in the budget – three million francs, as opposed to six and a half in an earlier version – meant that costs constantly had to be cut. These and other problems, however, only spurred Le Corbusier on to further experimentation; from this came studies carried out in various fields, such as drywall construction and sound-proofing.

Le Corbusier's modern methods triggered off a ferocious smear campaign in the Swiss press, which mistook the Pavillon's rationalist aims and the pristine simplicity of its materials, spaces and forms for empty materialism. The architect's detractors assured that this could only have a harmful effect on the young students. Once again, the use of exposed concrete and glass caused sparks to fly between Le Corbusier and his more obtuse critics. Finally, the addition of microscope images of natural subjects in the entrance hall was seen as conclusive proof of a mechanicist-scientific viewpoint tarnished by theoretical anti-humanism.

The *Gazette de Lausanne* published a dismissive article entitled 'Encore le Pavillon suisse', on 28 December 1933, with a bizarre interpretation of the photographs mounted on panels in the entrance hall. These reproduced details of natural forms, plants (cross-sections of trees, reeds and piles of logs) and animals (beehives, microphotographs of cells).

'But there is a theory behind these photographs. A materialistic theory: "everything depends on structure; nothing more nor less than the good organization of material". (The soul, and naturally the Spirit, are replaced by structure.)' (4)

Forms that require new decoding methods and create semantic conflicts almost inevitably suffer from kneejerk rejection as a result of incomprehension. This is a fairly common consequence of a lack of appropriate cultural codes to decipher new signs – either because these codes have yet to be created, or because they are still in the process of being assimilated and socially accepted. As new tools for interpretation are developed over time, these revolutionary forms become smootly integrated into the social world and the true value of their breadth of vision is finally recognized.

History shows us an unbroken string of buildings ahead of their time; one example among many is the Goldman & Salatsch Building, designed by Adolf Loos, in the Michaelerplatz in Vienna (1910), which was derided in its day but has since been recognized as part of the city's rich historic heritage. In the same way, the Pavillon Suisse has successfully transcended its time and space to become an architectural model and reference point – in short, one of the most lucid buildings of the twentieth century.

'The Pavillon Suisse has been described as one of the seminal buildings of the century, and it is true; its progeny are scattered all over the world, and number such distinguished buildings as Lever House in New York, the UN building, Lucio Costa's famous Ministry of Health and Education in Rio de Janeiro, and many other office blocks or public buildings....' (5)

Sources
(1) Reyner Banham, *Guide to Modern Architecture*, Princeton and New York, 1962, p. 108
(2) William J. R. Curtis, *Le Corbusier: Ideas and Forms*, London, 1986, p. 105
(3) Le Corbusier, *The Complete Architectural Works, vol. 2, 1929–1934,* London, 1964, p. 84
(4) Le Corbusier, *The Complete Architectural Works, vol. 2, 1929–1934,* p. 76
(5) Reyner Banham, *Guide to Modern Architecture*, p. 110–12

1

1 View of the north façade. The two concave volumes in the front contain the library – the lower section, in the foreground – and, behind it, the tower that holds the stairwell and other amenities. Behind them there stands a third volume, a pure prism, which holds the students' bedrooms. The form of the first two volumes resolves the meeting of the building and the access route, which is oblique in comparison to the general orientation. The two elements are further integrated by means of the roundabout.

2 and 3 Opposite: General view and detail of the south façade, with its panoramic views. The repeated modulation of the façade into forty-five windows – one for each student's room – alters at the top to indicate the presence of other facilities. The flat form and continuous grid of windows contrast with the rubble wall of the library and the sheets of natural stone on the stair tower, perforated with small openings. Le Corbusier acknowledged the various functions contained within the Pavillon by formally differentiating their corresponding volumes.

2

3

4

5

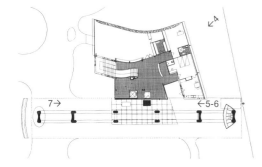

4 and 5 Partial view of the library and the entrance to the Pavillon. The glass lobby serves as a transition between the rectilinear residential block and the curved volume to the rear. The transparent sides allow sunshine to pour into the reception and their lightness contrasts with the solid opacity of the concrete.

6

7

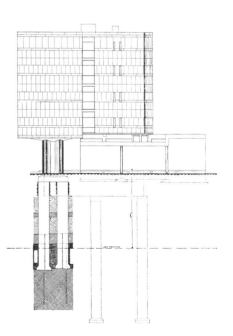

6 and 7 Views, from both ends, of the sturdy pilotis that raise and support the residential block. This technique frees the area under the concrete slabs, thereby creating – as would occur later in the Unité d'Habitation in Marseilles – not only a transit space but also a covered meeting point suitable for relaxation or intellectual discussions. This function was repeatedly suggested by Le Corbusier.

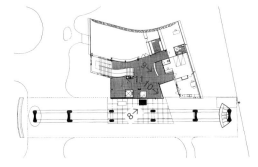

8, 9 and 10 Main entrance to the residence and different views of the communal entrance space (reception, waiting area and doorway).

11 Opposite: On the left, a lift, and, on the right, the staircase going up to the bedrooms. Alongside the stairs, the biconvex volume covered with photographs has heating pipes hidden in its interior. The irregular form of both the space in general and the staircase in particular reflect their role as spaces of confluence.

'The plan libre: *the pillars, the pipes, the curved walls and the staircase are all organs independent of each other.*'

12

13

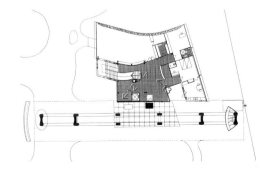

12 and 13 Furniture designed by the architect and a view of the lobby. The glass screen separating this area from the library fuses the two spaces visually, while its curved form echoes the contours of the library block.

14 Opposite: Detail of the staircase and lighting system. The curve runs parallel to that of the library.

15, 16, and 17 Views of the library. The mural was added later, between 1948 and 1949. It includes mythological references found elsewhere in Le Corbusier's work, such as a series of Symbolist elements, including the Open Hand motif and the Minotaur, mentioned in his *Poème de l'Angle Droit*. The mural also features lines from a poem by Mallarmé. Opposite, far right: facing the mural, the wall separating the library from the lobby; the glass wall on the top section serves to visually unite the two spaces.

'The extreme tightness of the budget made it necessary to reduce to the minimum all the dimensions, whatever they were. However, because of their deliberate distortions, the lobby and the library give the impression of having sufficient space.'

18

19

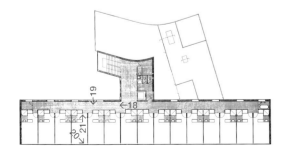

18 and 19 Corridor that connects the students' bedrooms. In contrast to the irregularities of the ground floor, which has a dynamism that reflects its status as a public and circulatory space, these spaces are formally neutral and rectilinear, with controlled openings. This change of emphasis heralds the entrance into a more private setting.

20

21

20 and 21 Interior of one of the bedrooms. View of the window on the south façade and, from there, view of the entrance. The austerity of the overall treatment is a reflection of the rigorous intellectual work undertaken here. The layout and design of the elements in the room are similar to those later found in the rugged cells of La Tourette monastery and in the hotel rooms in the Marseilles Unité.

duval factory

1951 saint-dié

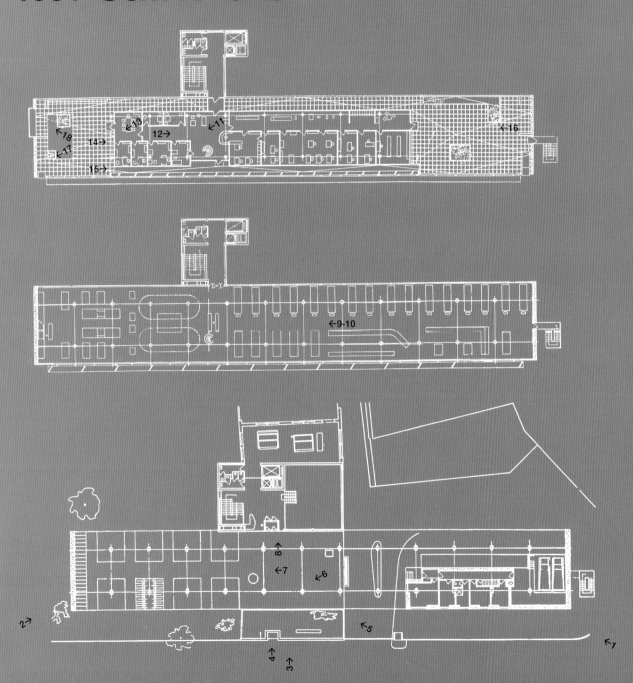

This was a commission from Jean-Jacques Duval, a knitwear manufacturer and friend of Le Corbusier. Back in 1945, Duval had already interceded with the local authorities on the architect's behalf in an attempt to win him the contract to rebuild the town of Saint-Dié, which had been damaged by several fires at the end of 1944, during its liberation by Allied troops. Le Corbusier began work on this project, but it was not brought to fruition due to the strong opposition of local architects and a good many of the inhabitants.

Le Corbusier, proposal for the reconstruction of Saint-Dié, 1945

Years later, in 1951, Duval commissioned him to rebuild his own factory. This had been partially destroyed in the fires, which had basically affected the front of the complex but left the rear intact. Working to the premise of respecting the surviving section, Le Corbusier set about designing a new building on the ruins of the old front section and even recycled material from the debris (the natural stone closing the sides of the new, rectangular structure). He linked the two volumes by means of a ground-floor reception area.

Silos and lifts for wheat in the US.

The Duval factory was Le Corbusier's first project after the war, and it allowed him to put to the test many of his ideas and theories on industrial buildings. It provided an unbeatable opportunity to demonstrate the essentiality of primary volumes that he had extolled in even his earliest writings:

'Without following any architectural idea, but simply guided by the results of calculations (derived from the principles governing our universe) and by the concept of a LIVING ORGANISM, today's ENGINEERS use primary elements and coordinate them in accordance with rules, instilling in us architectural emotions, thereby making human works resound to the rhythm of the universal order. We have only to look at the American silos and factories, magnificent FIRST FRUITS of the new age. AMERICAN ENGINEERS ARE OVERWHELMING OUR DYING ARCHITECTURE WITH THEIR CALCULATIONS.' (1)

At the same time, the factory was developed in accordance with the harmonic guidelines of the Modulor, which guaranteed the balance and proportion of all its components. This method was complemented by a meticulously ordered colour scheme on the ceilings (in striking contrast to the rough textures of the concrete), the woodwork and the services (blue for the plumbing, green for the air-conditioning ducts and yellow for the electrical fittings).

'...it has been possible to use a technique that is almost musical: counterpoint and fugue on the Modulor.' (2)

In effect, Le Corbusier treated and described the various architectural elements as components of a symphony, a chain of events running from the ground-floor access to the offices and roof terrace to form a self-sufficient and harmonious whole classified and enumerated by the architect.

*'There are three main masses:
The colonnade of exposed pillars;
The parallelepiped of the workshops;
The roof, with the offices and winter garden.*

*There are, moreover, three cadences, three different rhythms:
a) The intervals in the supporting frame of reinforced concrete: pilotis, uprights and floors;
b) The concrete grid of the* brise-soleil *on the façade of the workshops;
c) The trellis of the glass panels (with oak frames) that stretches behind the* brise-soleil, *in front of the workshops and offices.'* (3)

The pilotis supporting the building created a covered space – as is the case in the Unité in Marseilles, built at around the same time – which on this occasion was used to park bicycles. The workshop space was organized around an efficient production chain, from arrival of raw materials to assembly (cutting, knitting, ironing) and packaging of the end products and subsequent storage in the loading bays. In this setting, the ramp – the highlight of the architectural promenade – becomes a toboggan or chute that transports products from one space to another. Furthermore, the geometric lines of the *brise-soleil* on the workshops and the office volume on the roof emphasize the harmony and precise compositional rhythm running through the building's design. Le Corbusier uses all these elements to create a metaphor for basic mechanical efficiency, the 'producing machine' of the Duval factory. Le Corbusier was particularly satisfied with this work, as can be seen from the letter he wrote to his friend Jean-Jacques Duval on 13 December 1950:

'...we have made your factory a small masterpiece in the Florentine spirit...' (4)

The two men's close friendship – symbolized by Le Corbusier's status as godfather to Duval's son Rémy – was strengthened by their agreement on many issues, and it would be consolidated still further over the course of the years. Nevertheless, some misunderstandings did arise over the drawn-out construction period – three years – as a result of the complications inherent to the building. Several decisions aroused the fury of Le Corbusier, even though these did not come directly from Duval himself:

'I have given orders to your father to demolish the hideous wooden shack that has been built under the gallery in the large hall, as well as the absolutely ridiculous pigeonholes at the far end of the same room.' (5)

This fury was capable of blinding Le Corbusier to the visual harmony of the complex, with a subsequent danger of neutralizing its underlying overall vision and even overriding his own principles.

'Any visitor who sees the pigeonholes for fabric at the top of the gallery, or those that run along the ironing room at the height of the metal shaft on one of the double doors, would wonder what type of unpardonable negligence or thoughtlessness reigned in their architect.' (6)

In the main, however, the building work corresponded to the plans and the Duval factory became a magnificent example of a well-proportioned and functionally synchronized vessel, both in its forms – with the rich counterpoint between the rough cement and the colourful surfaces – and in its commitment to utilitarianism – a logical consequence of the manufacturing process.

'I can tell you, however, that your factory, because of the colours and the proportions that enliven it, will be remarkable.' (7)

Sources
(1) Le Corbusier, *Vers un architecture*, Paris, 1923
(2) Le Corbusier, *Le Modulor et Le Modulor 2*, Basel, 2000
(3) Le Corbusier, *Le Modulor et Le Modulor 2*, p. 149
(4) Jean Jenger (ed.), *Le Corbusier. Choix de lettres*, Basel, 2002, p. 332
(5) Jean Jenger (ed.), *Le Corbusier. Choix de lettres*, p. 332
(6) Jean Jenger (ed.), *Le Corbusier. Choix de lettres*, p. 333
(7) Jean Jenger (ed.), *Le Corbusier. Choix de lettres*, p. 333

'There are three main masses: the colonnade of exposed
pillars; the parallelepiped of the workshops; the roof,
with the offices and winter garden.'

1

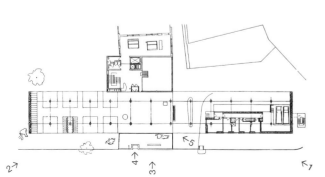

1 Previous page: Façade facing south-east, overlooking the street. The main block, newly built on the ruins of the old factory; natural stone was salvaged to close the rectangular box that forms the building. The top part contains the garden terrace and, on the left, the offices.

2 The west face, clad in stone like the façade on the opposite side. Both the textured surface of the material and the closed treatment of both sides contrast with the concrete grill of the new intervention. On the top left, the loggia on the garden terrace.

3 Detail of the main façade, which looks towards the south-east. The *brise-soleil* acts as a solar filter protecting the glass surface with the wooden framework.

4

5

4 Entrance to the factory, behind which lies the reception
   area, with the staircase that communicates with the upper
   floors. This space also serves as a link to the rear section of
   the building, which was spared by the fire that destroyed a
   large part of the factory.

5 In the foreground, an air duct, whose form, like other
   elements in the building, echoes the vocabulary of a ship –
   a metaphor for the efficient, self-sufficient vessel that the
   factory aspires to be. In the background, the row of sturdy
   pilotis that support the body of the building.

6 and 7 Views of the space that has been freed under the volume of the factory through the use of pilotis. The result is an area that can serve several different functions – for parking bicycles or receiving goods, for example. The severity of the concrete is offset by the colour applied to its surfaces.

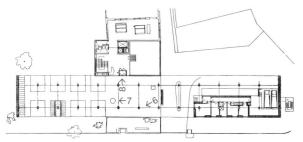

'I can tell you, however, that your factory, because of the colours
and the proportions that enliven it, will be remarkable.'

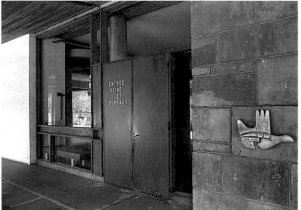

8

9

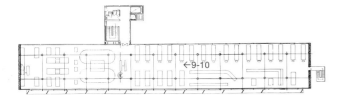

8 Entrance to the interior of the building, designed, like the entire factory, according to the Modulor system of proportions.

9 View of the assembly area and the upper gallery with the cutting department. This double-height space along the main façade benefits from ample natural light. The linear production methods used in the manufacturing process are paralleled by the quest for mechanical efficiency that underlies the architecture. The tubular forms of the handrails provide another naval reference.

10 As on the ground floor, the harshness of the concrete and
stone, which highlights the industrial nature of the building,
is alleviated by the colour scheme on the ceilings. This
strategy is continued elsewhere in the building and is even
applied to the plumbing and the electrical fittings.

11

12

11

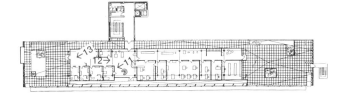

11 Reception and waiting room on the fourth floor, at the top of the building. In the background, a corridor with management offices and meeting rooms on the left and other administrative areas on the right.

12 Paintings by Le Corbusier – often blown-up details – cover the walls of both the hall and the offices.

13 Opposite: Interior of the meeting room, with a reproduction of the Modulor Man taken from the façade of the Marseilles Unité. The pivoting door makes the two spaces independent, while also serving as a noteboard.

14

15

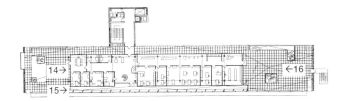

14: Detail of the *brise-soleil* in the area leading from the offices to the garden terrace; the screens can be pivoted to regulate the entrance of sunlight into the interior.

15 View of the two planes that form the southern façade of the offices; the series of concrete slabs on the right and the wooden framework on the left are separated by a narrow corridor.

16 Opposite: The garden terrace and the office block.

17

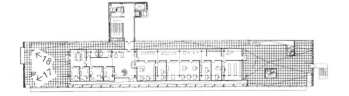

17 Garden terrace. Loggia built on the west side, with splendid views of Saint-Dié. The elegant orthogonal simplicity of its forms has a dynamic counterpoint in the small elements dotted around the space (concrete flower beds and geometrical forms).

18 Opposite: Far end of the loggia. Le Corbusier planned to insert a sculpture here (as seen in the sketch), but it was never actually made.

unité d'habitation
1947–52 marseilles

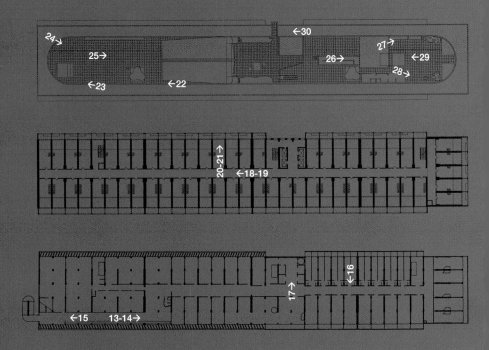

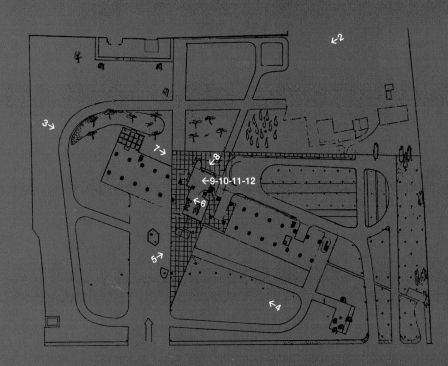

'Wogensky asked me what dimensions the first stone should have. I took the 2.26-m Modulor strip from my pocket and improvised, looking at the measurements and locating them between my outstretched hands:
Width...... 86 cm – Blue series
Height...... 86 cm – Blue series
Length...... 183 cm – Red series
...This great stone, consecrated eight days later, has dignity and elegance. It was also to give rise to an architectural improvisation to the greater glory of the Modulor.' (1)

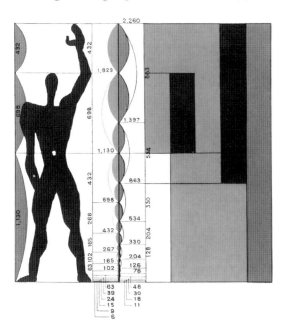

Le Corbusier, illustration of the Modulor system

Le Corbusier, Unité in Nantes, 1955

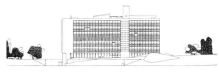

Le Corbusier, Unité in Berlin, 1957

Le Corbusier, Unité in Briey, 1961

Le Corbusier, Unité in Firminy, 1968

The Unité in Marseilles, the first and most complete of the five Unités d'Habitation à Grandeur Conforme (Dwelling Units of Congruent Size) built by Le Corbusier, was opened on 14 October 1952, exactly five years after the first stone was laid. This complex made the first extensive use of the Modulor system, which was used for everything, from the dimensions of the perimeter of the block, down to the smallest interior elements (both spatial and structural). The Marseilles experiment was followed by others in Rezé-les-Nantes, 1955; Berlin, 1957; Briey-en-Forêt, 1961 and Firminy-Vert, 1963–68.

This series of Unités was a response to the need for large-scale housing systems in France to alleviate the acute shortage after the destruction of the war.

'The Plan comprises 8 housing units destined to accommodate 20,000 people whose houses had been systematically destroyed in three days by the occupying force.' (2)

The Unité in Marseilles was intended to become a blueprint that could later be used in other cities. Its extraordinary dimensions were indicative of the urgent need for public housing.

'Built on the grass in the middle of an extensive park covering 3.5 hectares, bathed in sunlight, the Unité d'Habitation faces east–west and has no openings towards the north, the side exposed to the Mistral. Measurements: 165 m in length, 24 m in depth, 56 m in height. The building was built on pilotis. The ground is left free and available for pedestrian use. There is a car park and bicycle paths.' (3)

The commission was issued by two successive Ministers of Reconstruction, Raoul Dautry and Eugène Claudius-Petit, but it also required the support of no less than seven successive city councils to overcome the protests and vehement opposition of bodies such as the Société des Architectes Diplomés, the Conseil Supérieur de l'Hygiène and the Société pour l'Esthétique de la France. They tried to scupper the project with a flurry of arguments, ranging from alleged non-compliance with building regulations to the startling claim that future inhabitants of the Unité would be at risk of succumbing to mental illness.

Shortly afterwards, Le Corbusier recalled the conditions surrounding the construction process.

'I found myself in a pitched battle in Marseilles: 1946–52. The profession (the architects and their organizers) blocked the way. The Marseilles building was built on a battlefield.' (4)

In the Marseilles Unité, Le Corbusier transposed his thinking on individual housing to the context of collective living, inspired by his visit to the Charterhouse of Ema in 1907; he would further develop these ideas years later in the monastery of La Tourette. In his book *La Charte d'Athènes* (5), Le Corbusier discussed the need to find a harmony between the intrinsic human principles of the individual and the collective. In the same book, in the 'Observations and Requirements' attached to the sections *Habitation*, *Recreation, Work* and *Circulation*, he formulated principles that he would put into practice in Marseilles (reserving the ground space of high buildings for green areas, proximity of home and workplace, etc.). There were other precedents, too: the plans for the cities of Nemours, in Algeria, 1934, and Zlin, in Czechoslovakia, 1935, as well as the inevitable naval metaphors on display in Marseilles on both a formal and functional level (a building as a self-sufficient vessel).

Le Corbusier, town plan for the city of Nemours, Algeria, 1934

The various Unités involved the construction of several buildings that formed a complex surrounded by expansive green spaces for collective use.

Le Corbusier, regulatory plan for the Zlin Valley, Czechoslovakia, 1935

More specifically, the original Marseilles project – initially intended for the dock area of La Madraque – was planned to comprise a number of large blocks, two towers and several family houses. Together, they would form a residential setting made up of individual homes in the framework of a collective structure, following the model of the monastic lifestyle in the Charterhouse of Ema.

In the end, only one freestanding building was put up, on Boulevard Michelet; conceptually similar to the Pavillon Suisse, it stands on pilotis. It is distinguished by three horizontal planes of communication: the ground floor, articulated by the

Le Corbusier, early plan for the *Unité d'Habitation à grandeur conforme*, 1945

pilotis; the intermediate level, which serves as a 'street' with service facilities, and, on top, the shared terrace, which contains the rest of the communal services, all linked by the cluster of lifts. The latter are seen from the exterior as a vertical strip that culminates in a pure form on the terrace, a simple prism that contrasts with the horizontality that dominates the building.

The exposed concrete structure displays rough textures that reproduce the imperfections of the plank moulds used to make it. Once it was erected, prefabricated elements, including housing units, were fitted in, illustrating Le Corbusier's famous image of bottles placed in a rack. In fact, the building process was not conceived in this form, and concrete was only used instead of the originally planned steel because of the shortage of materials after the war, but Le Corbusier used it as an idiom to embody new emotions, drawing out all the beauty contained in its expressive primitivism.

'The construction of the Unité in Marseilles will bring to contemporary architecture the certainty of the splendour of reinforced concrete as an exposed material, on the same level as stone, wood and terracotta. The experiment is an important one. It truly seems possible to consider reinforced concrete as reconstituted stone, worthy of being displayed in its primary state.' (6)

Le Corbusier placed all the power supply equipment together in the entrails of the building. The *terrain artificiel* (artificial ground) is a thoroughfare that provides access to the Unité's nervous system and makes it easy to locate machinery, pipes and shafts, so that any breakdown can be dealt with immediately.

'The artificial ground on top of the pilotis is a plane 135 metres long and 24 metres wide; it rests on the pilotis of 17 porticos 8.38 metres apart. The pilotis are made of concrete and their form is a response to their function: stability for the building and conduits for the plumbing. The artificial ground is made up of 32 compartments containing mechanical equipment: on the left, the ventilation machinery and, on the right, the air ducts that branch off to individual floors, along with the main sewage pipes.' (7)

The importance given to the accessibility and smooth functioning of this space in Le Corbusier's detailed description is not unwarranted, given the building's size and complexity – it was intended to house around 1,600 people, a figure very similar to that of the Phalanstère, designed by the utopian socialist Charles

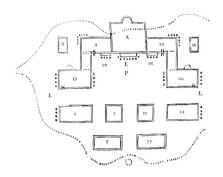

Charles Fourier, general plan of the Phalanstère

Fourier. In order to cater for both the large number of inhabitants and their diverse lifestyles, the Marseilles Unité contained a total of 337 apartments of 23 distinct types, spread over 17 storeys. Apart from those situated on the southern façade, they all enjoy views on two sides (of the mountains to the east and the sea to the west).

The wide range of different apartments meant that each one could be adapted to the specific requirements of their inhabitants; the options included individual apartments for students, homes for families with up to ten members and hotel rooms. The interiors followed the criteria formulated for the Maison Citrohan, with large windows and a double-height living room – bounded but also visually enriched by a terrace – along with an open-plan kitchen and a bedroom on the upper floor. The double-height residential cells were juxtaposed in section and access was provided by internal 'streets' set on every third floor.

'The internal street is in reality an extraordinary and mysterious symphony of colours.' (8)

The homes were christened *logements prolongés* ('extended dwellings'), in reference to the twenty-six communal services — *services communs de ravitaillement* — on offer to residents. Most of these are situated on the shopping street on the intermediate level, distinguished from the outside by the parallel vertical strips running along it. The thin glass skin on the interior, behind the *brise-soleil* of the strips, gives rise to remarkable, ever-changing lighting effects that recall the movement inherent to this communication space. The street is filled with shops, offices and other services which, although failing to satisfy all the expectations of the initial project, do allow the inhabitants to do much of their day-to-day shopping.

'Halfway up (levels 7 and 8) is the shopping street for provisions (communal services), which includes: shops for fish, charcuterie, meat, groceries, wine, dairy products, fruit and vegetables, as well as a bakery and a shop selling prepared dishes. Delivery to one's apartment can be arranged. A restaurant, tea room, and snack bar provide meals.' (9)

The *brise-soleil* wall also continues the pattern of the glass curtain wall to the rear of the homes, where sunlight is prevented from entering directly in summer but is allowed to penetrate in winter, with the interior space serving as a filter to the terrace.

Finally, the Unité's roof is the location of the remaining communal facilities: the kindergarten, with a small swimming pool, the gym, the running track and the open-air theatre are all elements that promote a healthy life under the open skies, free from city traffic and in contact with nature.

'The roof terrace, which is both a hanging garden and a belvedere, provides a gymnasium, an open-air space for training and gymnastics, a solarium, a 300-metre running track, a buffet-bar, etc.' (10)

The sculptural monumentality of the ventilation ducts, which echo the form of the pilotis on the ground floor, the striking setting of the theatre and the truncated geometry of the lift shaft add the finishing touches to this stage for new, modern rituals.

'A symphony of forms with the intensity in the exact spot (which serves as a base for the mountains on the horizon): creation of an oblique, regulated surface and, likewise, the creation of "dromedaries": two hollow concrete elements that act as a barrier between the track and the children's play area.' (11)

A brick parapet blocks off the immediate surroundings and directs the gaze onto the distant views of the mountain and the sea.

'The space was too extensive, the horizon was uninteresting, a wall was put up on the right, and three steps at the back.' (12)

The elements distributed over the social setting formed by the Unité's terrace – from the kindergarten to the gymnasium, from the theatre to the running track – bring together inhabitants of all age groups, and so reflect every stage of human life. Furthermore, Le Corbusier replied to criticism of the imperfections in the concrete finishing by metaphorically defining the surface of the terrace as a human skin that, by its nature, must bear witness to the passing of time.

'When you look at men and women, can't you see that they have wrinkles, marks, a nose with defects, countless accidents?' (13)

For this reason, Le Corbusier, aware of the impossibility of controlling the finishing and making it uniform, used the imperfections inherent in the building system, such as deformations in the wood of the plank moulds, as textures with distinct expressive characteristics. The roughness and protuberances of the cement became distinguishing traits that asserted the aesthetic value of its intrinsic coarseness.

'The ramp on the roof, with its deformations that are impossible to rectify, serves as a starting point for architectural contrasts: the slenderness of the iron railings, the polychrome of the tiles.' (14)

Contrasts are present in a wide range of sequences, both in the Unité and in Le Corbusier's earlier buildings, usually as an expression of the dualistic dynamic typical of his work. At times, however – as when he added colour to the sides of terraces – it became a device to reduce the impact of errors in the finishing or the proportions.

'It is the effect of this unfortunate design that has given rise to the addition of polychrome to the façades, intended to distract the eye.' (15)

Be that as it may, the dialogue between expressive artistic forms and the play of sunshine is extremely forceful. These ubiquitous forms are disparate and visually distinctive but they are united by the proportioned geometry of the Modulor, persistently calling to mind the emotional sense of one of the declarations that best encapsulated Le Corbusier's thinking:

'Architecture is the magnificent, masterly and correct play of volumes under light.' (16)

Sources
(1) Le Corbusier, *Le Modulor et Le Modulor 2*, Basel, 2000
(2) Le Corbusier, *The Complete Architectural Works, vol. 5, 1946–1952*, London, 1970, p. 190
(3) Le Corbusier, *The Complete Architectural Works, vol. 5, 1946–1952*, p. 194
(4) Le Corbusier, *Le Modulor et Le Modulor 2*, p. 310
(5) Le Corbusier, *La Charte d'Athènes*, Paris, 1943
(6) Le Corbusier, *The Complete Architectural Works, vol. 5, 1946–1952*, p. 190
(7) Le Corbusier, *The Complete Architectural Works, vol. 5, 1946–1952*, p. 199
(8) Le Corbusier, *The Complete Architectural Works, vol. 5, 1946–1952*, p. 205
(9) Le Corbusier, *The Complete Architectural Works, vol. 5, 1946–1952*, p. 194
(10) Le Corbusier, *The Complete Architectural Works, vol. 5, 1946–1952*, p. 194
(11) Le Corbusier, *The Complete Architectural Works, vol. 5, 1946–1952*, p. 221
(12) Le Corbusier, *The Complete Architectural Works, vol. 5, 1946–1952*, p. 222
(13) Le Corbusier, *The Complete Architectural Works, vol. 5, 1946–1952*, p. 190
(14) Le Corbusier, *The Complete Architectural Works, vol. 5, 1946–1952*, p. 214
(15) Le Corbusier, *The Complete Architectural Works, vol. 5, 1946–1952*, p. 200
(16) Le Corbusier, *Vers un architecture*, Paris, 1923

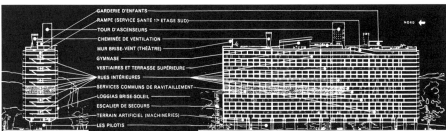

GARDERIE D'ENFANTS
RAMPE (SERVICE SANTÉ 17ª ETAGE SUD)
TOUR D'ASCENSEURS
CHEMINÉE DE VENTILATION
MUR BRISE-VENT (THÉÂTRE)
GYMNASE
VESTIAIRES ET TERRASSE SUPÉRIEURE
RUES INTÉRIEURES
SERVICES COMMUNS DE RAVITAILLEMENT
LOGGIAS BRISE-SOLEIL
ESCALIER DE SECOURS
TERRAIN ARTIFICIEL (MACHINERIES)
LES PILOTIS

NORD

'Built on the grass in the middle of an extensive park covering 3.5 hectares [8½ acres], bathed in sunlight, the Unité d'Habitation faces east–west and has no openings towards the north, the side exposed to the Mistral.'

2

1 Previous page: View of the east façade overlooking the
Boulevard Michelet. The nucleus of staircases and lifts can
be seen as a vertical element in the façade and ends on the
roof in the form of a prism. The internal street halfway up the
building is indicated on the outside by a horizontal streak
protected by a series of vertical concrete strips.

2 West façade, with the internal street of communal facilities,
including a small restaurant at one end.

3

4

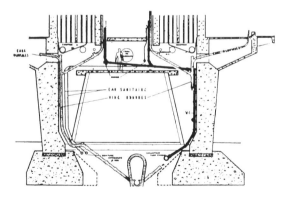

3   Partial view of the south-facing side. The building
is supported by sturdy troncoconical pilotis, leaving
a large free space underneath. The model for this
suspended box was the Pavillon Suisse, built twenty
years earlier in the Cité Universitaire in Paris.

4   East façade. The building's entire nervous system is
concentrated under the building, in the 'artificial ground',
a thoroughfare with access to machinery and equipment.

*'The artificial ground is made up of 32 compartments containing
mechanical equipment: on the left, the ventilation machinery and, on the
right, the air ducts that branch off to individual floors, along with the main
sewage pipes.'*

5

6

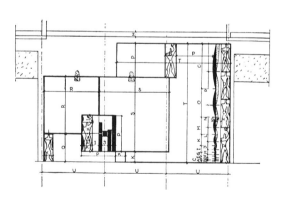

5 The blind wall hiding the lift shaft is divided into geometric sections of various sizes; Le Corbusier added a moulded Modulor figure, the system of proportions applied to all internal and external dimensions of the Unité.

6 View from the lobby showing the space underneath the building, which is open to a variety of uses (parking for bicycles, play area, etc.).

7

8

7   West façade. The block that houses the entrance to the building's lobby, wedged underneath the *terrain artificiel*, with an overhang on the left, and large window on the right.

8   Main entrance to the Unité. The artificial lighting enhances the rustic opacity of the concrete around the taut transparency of the glass. In contrast to the sunshine that penetrates in the daytime and reflects off the Travertine floor, the artificial lighting modulates the interior space in a balanced fashion and projects the volumes outwards.

'Violent contrasts between the flawless Securit windows and the exposed concrete.'

9

←9-10-11-12

'The lobby. Combination of artificial light and natural light.'

9 General view of the lobby. The contrast between the intense sunshine outside and the subdued lighting inside, between nature and orthogonal geometry, emphasizes the difference between the two settings.

10

11

12

10 and 11 The formal expressiveness of the cracked, slightly curved pilotis is enhanced by the lighting from below. The pane of glass on which they seem to rest gives them a tense weightlessness that belies their function as supports. The pilotis also act as a filter, a partial screen anticipating the cement wall to their rear.

12 A coloured glass design set in the wall of the lobby is an attempt to create 'a new kind of stained glass, free of leading and imbued with the spirit of the age', in the words of Le Corbusier himself. Stained glass would later acquire a special emotional impact in Ronchamp, showing 'that architecture is not a matter of columns, but one of evocative events'.

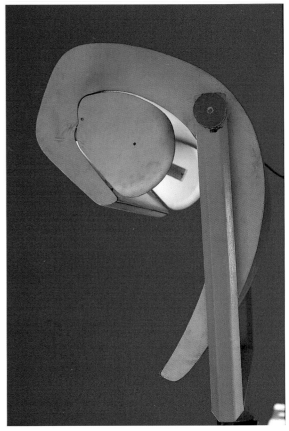

14

13 The internal shopping street, with its double height, houses the communal facilities for the residents – the *services communs de ravitaillement*. The street is enclosed by a thin skin of glass, within a *brise-soleil* made up of vertical concrete strips.

14 Detail of one of the lamps on the internal street. Set against the opaque planes of the street, its organic form stands out sharply in a setting otherwise dominated by straight lines. Its reflected light similarly contrasts with the direct light pouring in from outside.

15 View of the other end of the internal street (the north façade). The sunlight is filtered through both the *brise-soleil* and the glass pane to create an extraordinary pattern of light and shade on the floor that changes constantly, enlivening and expressing the personality of this communication space.

16

17

16 A bedroom in the Unité's hotel. As he often did, Le Corbusier reused a tried and tested solution, and this room is almost identical to the cells of the monastery of La Tourette. The cupboard hides a washing area with a small basin and shower.

17 Lift door in the corridor with entrances to the residences. This apparently neutral space is personalized by the materials used and their sheen in the sunlight, along with the colours on the woodwork.

18

19

'The internal street is in reality an extraordinary and mysterious symphony of colours.'

18 and 19 Corridor with access to the apartments and detail of one of the doors. The bright colour applied to each entrance and the strong individual lighting combine to project a delicate rainbow on the ceiling, thereby supplementing the diffuse lighting in this shadowy collective area. The small volume alongside each door is intended to receive post and small objects, which can be collected from indoors.

20

21

20 Interior of one of the duplex apartments, with the entrance staircase leading to the upper level. In the background, the front door and, on the right, a furniture unit with a hatch linking the kitchen and the dining room.

21 Two children's bedrooms, separated by a sliding partition that makes it possible to join the spaces into a single playroom. (Both of these photos were taken in the Nantes Unité, but the spaces are the same as those in Marseilles.)

22 The building's roof, which is the location of some of the communal facilities. The sculptural ventilation ducts reiterate the Unité's metaphorical link with shipping, also recalled by the tubular handrails and other elements. In the foreground, the running track that circles the edge of the terrace. In the background, the stage of the open-air theatre.

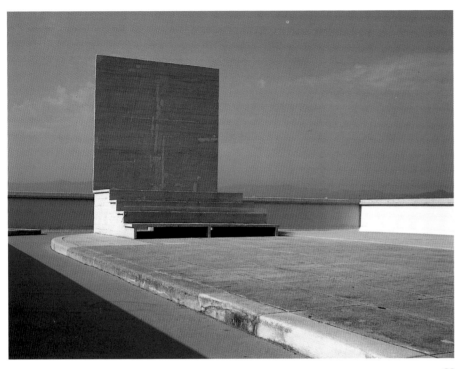

23

24

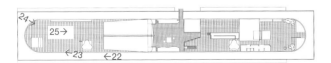

23 and 24 Views of the area allocated for open-air performances. A wall encloses the entire perimeter of the terrace; its great height isolates the building from nearby references, while leaving open the spectacular views of the mountains and sea in the distance ('one of the most grandiose and moving views in the world', according to Le Corbusier). The visual introversion establishes a distance from the hubbub on the streets below and allows residents to enjoy contact with nature.

25 Gymnasium, ventilation duct, plant display, lift shaft: all these volumes are proportioned according to the blue and red Modulor series. This approach serves to unify them, despite their marked formal differences and spatial dispersion. The multi-coloured facade of the gym contrasts with the roughness of the concrete and the finishings in general.

'The roof terrace, which is both a hanging garden and a belvedere, provides a gymnasium, an open-air space for training and gymnastics, a solarium, a 300-metre running track, a buffet-bar, etc.'

26

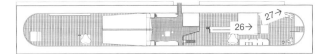

26 Small children's swimming pool, proportioned longitudinally
with the red series of the Modulor and transversally with the
blue series. The oblique surface of the ramp is bounded by
artificial rocks on both sides.

27 The concrete rocks are a replica of the mountains in the distance; the two are directly related visually, as the high walls block out the intervening landscape and seemingly bridge the distance between them. Le Corbusier later placed a similar element by the entrance to La Tourette, as both a reference and a homage to the monastery's natural surroundings.

'A symphony of forms with the intensity in the exact spot (which serves as a base for the mountains on the horizon): creation of an oblique, regulated surface and, likewise, the creation of "dromedaries": two hollow concrete elements that act as a barrier between the track and the children's play area.'

28

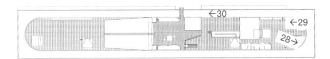

'Architecture is the magnificent, masterly and correct play of volumes under light.'

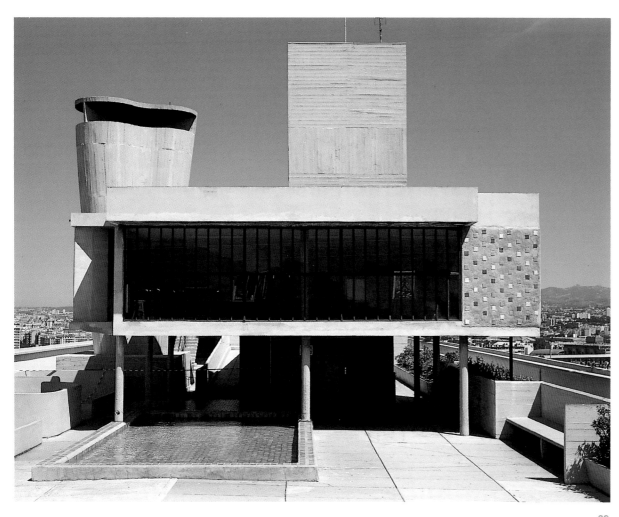

28 Opposite: The ramp, delimited by the enclosing wall and its ending beside the artificial rock. The whole ensemble, with the mountains in the distance, seems to change constantly according to the position of the sun, perfectly illustrating the statement by Le Corbusier quoted opposite.

29 In the foreground, the raised kindergarten, with one end of the small swimming pool set underneath, to provide protection from the sun. In the background, a ventilation duct and the slender prism of the lift shaft.

30 Staircase leading to the lifts and a spectacular balcony suspended above the running track.

la tourette
monastery
1957–60 eveux-sur-l'arbresle

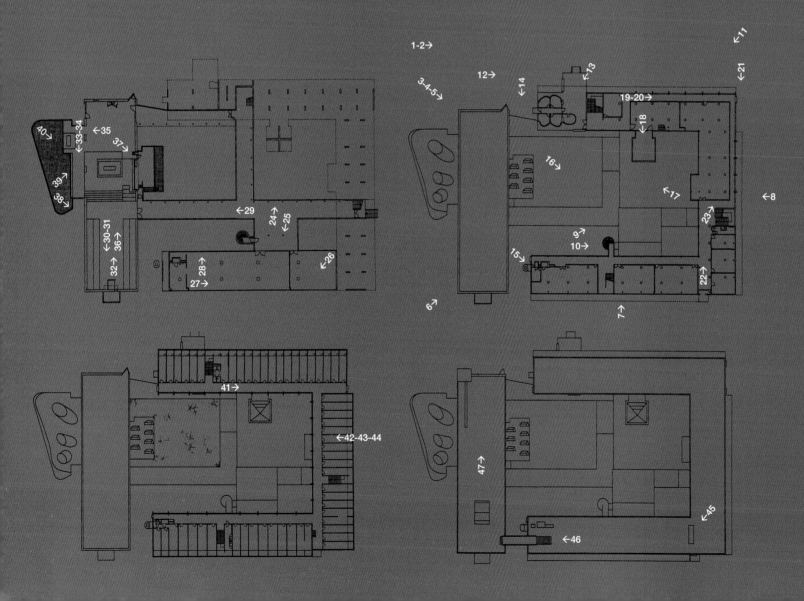

The essence of Le Corbusier's commission was conveyed poetically in these terms by his friend Father Marie-Alain Couturier, a Dominican who was a champion of modern art and editor of the journal *L'Art sacré*, and who had collaborated with artists including Chagall, Léger and Ozenfant. This succinct and heartfelt brief reveals the order's total confidence in Le Corbusier's ideas – and, therefore, in the forms derived from rationalism – over and above any other considerations, such as the requirements of the programme and the architectural

Cloister of the Cistercian monastery in Le Thoronet, Provence

preferences expressed by the monks (such as the Cistercian monastery in Le Thoronet, Provence: 'A monastery in its pure state'). Along with the then unfinished church in Ronchamp and the major projects of the Unités, La Tourette is proof of the acceptance of the modernist school in many socially influential circles: private enterprise, the political class (public housing) and the clergy.

La Tourette is, in effect, a magnificent example of post-war modern architecture, as well as being a treatise on light and – as is to be expected with Le Corbusier – a continuing series of dualities. To achieve these qualities, Le Corbusier scrupulously fulfilled the demands of the monastic lifestyle, both in general terms (layout) and on an individual level (dimensions and handling of the cells), described in detail by Couturier.

'According to the traditional plan, three large volumes should be set around the cloister: that of the church; in front, the refectory (demolished in Le Thoronet); on the third side, the chapter house and, finally, on the fourth side, two large meeting rooms. On the first floor, a big library. The rest of the building must be taken up by cells and other, medium-sized rooms.' (2)

In the same way, the expressive rawness of the materials not only corresponds to specific requirements but also constitutes an imposing metaphor for Dominican austerity: exposed, untreated cement; rough stone on the prefabricated (but seemingly handmade) elements in the exterior walls of the cell galleries; and service equipment left open to view.

'For us, the poverty of the construction must be very strict, without any element of luxury or superfluity, and this implies, as a result, that vital needs are respected: silence, a temperature sufficient for continuous intellectual work, comings and goings reduced to the minimum.' (3)

The monastery, some fifteen miles to the north-east of Lyons, is set on a hillside and reproduces the traditional format revolving around an inner cloister. Le Corbusier took into account not only Le Thoronet but also the Charterhouse of Galluzo in Tuscany, which he had seen on his travels as a young man and which

Charles-Édouard Jeanneret, sketch of the Galluzo monastery

he referred to by the Carthusian name of Ema. La Tourette also recalls the galleries in the Unités (Marseilles, Nantes), while the design of the cells reproduces almost exactly the model of the Marseilles hotel rooms and, finally, *pans de verre* (glass curtain walls) similar to those projected for the monastery were, at that very moment, being built in Chandigarh.

'The pans de verre situated above the three exterior façades make use, for the first time, of the system of "Pan de verre ondulatoire" (which has also been applied in the Secretariat of Chandigarh).' (4)

This mature work from Le Corbusier synthesizes, not for the first time, earlier experiments in new functional contexts. This approach was influenced by the fact that he was handling several projects at the same time, such as the Parliament Building, Secretariat and Capitol in Chandigarh (India), along with the Shodhan and Sarabhai Villas in Ahmedabad and, in Europe, the Villa Jaoul and the Unités in Berlin and Nantes, as well as the final stages of the Ronchamp chapel. This situation obliged Le Corbusier to divide his energies, but it also allowed him to remain open to experimentation, juxtaposition and interchange of ideas.

Furthermore, aside from his professional commissions, Le Corbusier also continued his intensive theoretical and literary work by participating in the *Congrès International d'Architecture Moderne* (CIAM) exhibiting his work in several countries, giving lectures and directing seminars. The pressure of work led him to delegate the supervision of several projects to Iannis Xenakis, whose musical and scientific training – he composed music based on mathematical

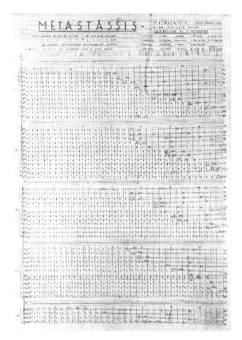

Iannis Xenakis, fragment of the composition *Metastasis*

principles – would be crucial to the definition of the rhythmic compositions of the *pans de verre*.

'This tangency of music and architecture, evoked on countless occasions in relation to the Modulor, is now consciously expressed in a musical score by Xenakis: Metastasis, *composed with the Modulor, which lent its resources to musical composition.'* (5)

It is this context of past and present experiments that enables us to understand and define La Tourette as a synthesis that is open, complex and dense, as a dazzling interplay between the emotional and the cerebral that earns it a place among Le Corbusier's most important projects.

'He is one of the few architects who have suppressed the demands of neither sensation nor thought. Between thought and sensation he has always maintained a balance; and therefore – and almost with him alone – while the intellect civilizes the sensible, the sensible actualizes civility.' (6)

This balance of opposites can be discerned in the approach to the monastery. The first element to come into view is the enormous vertical box that defines the church, a blind concrete surface embedded into the ground. This contrasts with the transparent horizontality of the three sides of the U-shape that form the monastery area and complete the square of the complex. The contrast between these two volumes is visually enhanced by the separation of their respective masses, thereby emphasizing the difference between the public space – the church has an independent entrance for the congregation – and the private space (the monastic life that is centred around the cloister).

Similarly, the layout and treatment of the elevation in the monastery's inner spaces reflect its various functions, as well as the duality of the communal and individual identities inherent to monastic life. This duality is further highlighted by the modular repetition of the cells – complete with galleries framing glimpses of the rugged landscape – and, in contrast, the presence of open spaces (refectory, halls, etc.). These two types of setting are complemented by other, clearly differentiated spaces devoted to prayer (altars in the crypt, the oratory), so the three strands of Dominican life – the social, individual and spiritual – are condensed into one.

The cells occupy the two upper floors and run along the perimeter of the U-shape; they are protected from the sun by a small gallery which, as mentioned above, looks out on the surrounding landscape. The cells' limited dimensions, the harsh rusticity of their walls and meagreness of their accessories – washbasin, cupboard, bed, table, chair and lamp – embody a fundamental expression of monastic life, forming a compendium of the monks' radical austerity and an unequivocal affirmation of sacrifice as their identifying principle. This is perfectly reflected in this description by a novice monk:

'The hardness of the white wall, the poverty of the furnishings stripped to the essentials and the general bareness should allow one to guess what is going to happen here: a hand-to-hand fight.' (7)

The cells are set above the communal areas (refectory, library, halls and several meeting and work rooms, along with the usual service facilities). These are all interrelated by an extensive communications system running through the entire building: long, narrow corridors, gentle ramps, a bridge at the entrance to the monastery, a rooftop walkway linking it to the church, and staircases of various shapes and sizes. These elements take on a personality of their own and, like a nervous system, unify the different sections of the monastery, thereby illustrating the open and receptive spirit of its inhabitants.

There is a tense relationship between individual parts and the whole, as a dynamic dialogue is established between the general and the particular, through the striking contrast between the overall structure of the complex – a static, clear-cut square – and the addition of various incorporated elements, all with a strong visual impact. These include the bell tower; the spiral staircase; the oratory for the novices; the angular crypt (a connection between nature and artifice) and the tapered space for the organ, both protuberances jutting out of the façades of the church; the dramatic walkway linking the monastery with the church; the stairwell going up to the roof; the sacristy, crowned with 'cannons of light', and the distinctive window casings (*fleurs de ventilation*).

As regards the church, the enigmatic nature of its introverted northern façade has been aptly compared by Colin Rowe to a work from the early part of Le Corbusier's career, the Villa Schwob, where the privileged central position of the blind panel disconcertingly invades the visual field, without ever proclaiming its presence.

Charles-Édouard Jeanneret, Villa Schwob, La Chaux-de-Fonds, 1916

'In 1916, at La Chaux-de-Fonds, Le Corbusier erected a house with a centrally disposed blank panel. Forty years later, and at a heroic scale, he has repeated something very like this device. At La Chaux-de-Fonds, the blank panel is the central figure of a façade. At La Tourette, a largely blank wall comprises the north side of the church.' (8)

The decisive simplicity of the exterior is endowed with dynamism in the interior by the placement and form of the elements set against the walls. Thus, the strict geometry of the main altar displays its symbolic relevance, as it lies in the intersection of the church's axes, adjacent to the sacristy (a formally autonomous element with a curved red surface that gleams with the sunshine entering through the holes in the ceiling, the 'cannons of light', aligned with the summer solstice). The other focus of attention is the pit of the crypt, whose bright yellow wall reflects the dramatic light pouring in through the cannons of light.

The colourful, narrow horizontal slits that allow sunlight to penetrate at the height of the benches – to facilitate reading – and the small skylight that breaks up the church's imposing verticality are further syntactic components of Le Corbusier's distinctive and exciting vocabulary, and the powerful sonority of their names emphasizes their leading role in a work that packs such a strong emotional punch.

'As you will have realized, I use light in abundance; for me, light is the fundamental basis of architecture. I compose with light.' (9)

As in the case of the church, the walls of the refectory, study halls and communication areas, with their irregular partitioning, use several different lighting systems that constantly modify the perception of space. So, the *pans de verre* – basically expanses of glass, but interspersed with blind panels – are composed horizontally in accordance with the Modulor red series and vertically in a three-part division, while the narrow slits of light from the corridors of the cells correspond to the blue series.

This system of proportions acquires a literally musical elegance and rhythm in the *ondulatoires*, a derivation of the *pans de verre*, glazing with concrete mullions running from floor to ceiling, separated from each other in accordance with a mathematically based musical composition by Xenakis. The short distances between the mullions create an impression of enclosure when seen head-on, disrupting the continuity of the exterior landscape, while an approach from an angle obscures the filtration of sunlight to give the appearance of a blind wall.

'So, the problem of lighting is always the same: knowing what lighting is. It is the walls that receive light. The illuminated walls. The emotion comes from what the eyes see – that is, the volumes – from what the body receives through the impression or pressure of the walls on it and then what the lighting gives you, whether in intensity or in softness, according to the places in which it is produced.' (10)

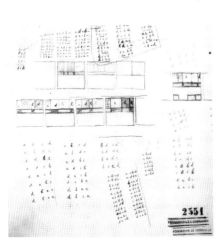

Iannis Xenakis, rhythmic composition of the *pans de verre* and *ondulatoires*

Finally, the roof displays a similar treatment to the experiment at the Unité d'Habitation in Marseilles: a surface that can be walked on but that is surrounded by a high wall enclosing the perimeter and isolating it from the immediate surroundings. The result is an immaterial void, removed from any physical references other than the chimney, the bell tower, the walkway and the top of the access staircase; these are the only elements that punctuate the space and accompany the monks in their intense meditation.

'Both the roof of the monastery and that of the church are covered with a thin layer of earth left to the mercy of the wind, the birds and other transporters of seeds, ensuring a watertight and isothermal protective cover.' (11)

Sources
(1) Sergio Ferro, Chérif Kebbal, Philippe Potié and Cyrille Simonnet, *Le Corbusier. Le couvent de la Tourette*, Marseilles, 1987, p. 12
(2) Jean Petit, *Un couvent de Le Corbusier*, Paris, 2001, p. 22. (Letter from R. P. Couturier to Le Corbusier, 23 July 1953)
(3) Jean Petit, *Un couvent de Le Corbusier*, p. 26
(4) Jean Petit, *Un couvent de Le Corbusier*, p. 111
(5) Le Corbusier, *Le Modulor et Le Modulor 2*, Basel, 2000
(6) Colin Rowe, *The Mathematics of the Ideal Villa and Other Essays*, Cambridge, Mass., 1976, p. 196
(7) Jean Petit, *Un couvent de Le Corbusier*, p. 74
(8) Colin Rowe, *The Mathematics of the Ideal Villa and other Essays*, Cambridge, Mass., 1976, p. 186
(9) Le Corbusier, *Précisions sur un état présent de l'architecture et de l'urbanisme*, Paris, 1960
(10) Jean Petit, *Un couvent de Le Corbusier*, p. 29
(11) Jean Petit, *Un couvent de Le Corbusier*, p. 111

1

2

3

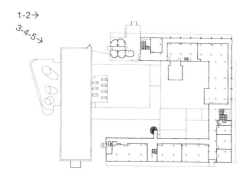

1-2→
3-4-5→

1 In line with Le Corbusier's usual practice, the approach road to the monastery does not stop at the main entrance but continues through the woods.

2 The monastery is glimpsed between the trees that line the road. Before reaching the main entrance, the road opens on to another route that goes down to the door of the church.

3 This deviation from the main road transfers visual attention to the right to reveal the immense blind rectangle of the side of the church.

4 North-east view, with the modular fragmentation of
the openings of the cells on the left and, on the right, the
volume of the church, which displays a sculptural, tapered
bell tower on the top and a curvilinear volume protruding
from the front.

5 The crypt contrasts with the unsettling blind wall of the
church and its varied, curved forms provide a transition
between the natural surroundings and the severe geometry
of the enclosed building. On the left, a direct access
route to the church enables the public to attend religious
ceremonies without disturbing the privacy of monastic life.

6

7

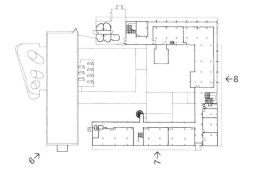

←8

6↗

7↗

6 North-west view, with the two volumes that make up the monastery. On the left, the church, a blind rectangle with elements such as the crypt and organ incorporated into the structure. On the right, the sharply contrasting U-shape that completes the square of the complex. The front of this volume, open to the landscape, contains the kitchens, refectory and halls on the ground floor, with the monk's cells on the top two storeys. The tension between the two surfaces is accentuated by the vertical gap, only broken on the top by the walkway leading to the garden terrace.

7 The building does not make direct contact with the ground in the kitchen section; a gap of just a few centimetres is enough to proclaim the building's desire for independence from its surroundings.

8

8   The south face makes more explicit the relationship
     between the building and its surroundings: the bold
     horizontality of the monastery asserts itself unperturbed
     by the contours of the hillside, which is only marked
     topographically by the progressive lengthening of the
     supporting pilotis. The spaces on this façade are
     differentiated according to their function: monastic
     cells for individual use, as opposed to the continuous
     treatment of the communal areas.

'The building has been conceived from the top: the composition begins with the line of the roof, a large, overall horizontal line, to define the gradient of the base on which the construction stands by means of pilotis.'

9

10

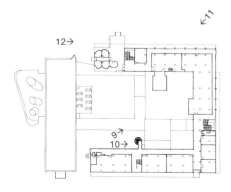

9 Partial view of the pilotis on which the building rests. The irregular gradient runs underneath the monastery, but without blending into it, thereby maintaining the building's independence from its surroundings.

10 The cylinder containing the spiral staircase is one of the monastery's most striking elements; its dynamism contrasts with the static uniformity of the building's square outline.

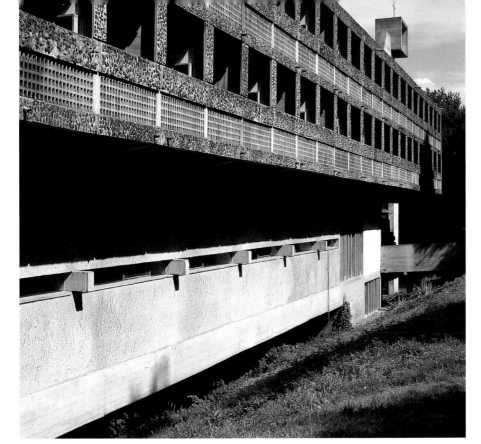

11 The east façade, running parallel to the access road, contains the main entrance to the monastery. The continuous, horizontal gap running along the façade marks the presence of an uninterrupted communication space within. Above this, the fronts of the cells, with their harsh rusticity, reflect the austerity of monastic life.

12 Walkway leading into the monastery; once again, the ground is left exposed and direct contact is avoided. In the foreground, two curved, independent volumes attract the eye; they were originally used as a reception area and a meeting point for monks and visitors.

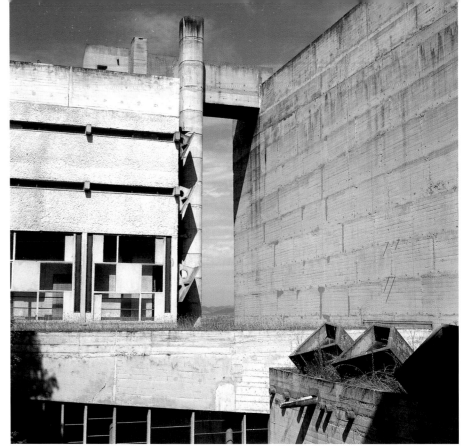

14

15

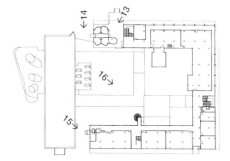

14 The bench and rock that mark the entrance to the building are sculptural pieces in their own right, over and above any particular function. Rocks are a recurring element in Le Corbusier's vocabulary, reappearing, for example, on the garden terrace of the Marseilles Unité, as a symbolic echo of the mountains in the distance. In La Tourette, they also provide a link with the lush landscape surrounding the monastery.

15 Meeting point of the church and the monastery itself. The walkway to the terrace garden connects the two volumes and provides access to the bell tower. This illustrates, once again, the contrast between the enigmatic immutability of the church wall and the diversity of the openings in the common spaces (the *pans de verre* and the horizontal light strips, designed in accordance with the red and blue Modulor series, respectively).

16 The view of the walkway from the ground highlights the tension of the space between the monastery and the church. The ventilation duct adds to the calculated spectacle of this area.

17 The cloister. Below, the *ondulatoires* in the communication areas (leading to the church and refectory) and the spiral staircase. Above, the *pans de verre* and the horizontal openings of the corridors that connect the cells.

18

19

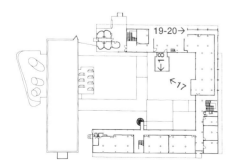

'La Tourette monastery is a spiritual, organically alive dwelling place, whose various parts are very different from each other but are closely connected.'

20

21

18 Opposite: The cloister. In the foreground, the novices' oratory, based on the juxtaposition of various geometrical solids (cross, cube, pyramid); in the background, the organic volumes of the reception area.

19 Opposite: Interior of the novices' oratory. The slits on the sides and in the top of the pyramid throw light on the rough walls and add a dramatic touch to the interior.

20 Communication space on the ground floor of the east façade. The horizontal strip of light, situated at eye level and calculated by means of the Modulor, runs along the entire corridor, setting up a contrast with the verticality of the space. The lighting, of course, varies throughout the day, depending on the position of the sun.

21 The *fleur de ventilation* in front of the window impedes the entrance of sunshine and air, as well as blocking the view, so the window's sole function is to light up the interior.

22

23

24

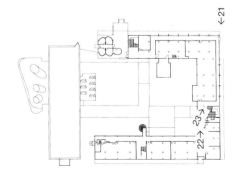

22 A *fleur de ventilation* seen from the exterior. These are
    proportioned in accordance with the Modulor – the smallest
    with the blue series, and the largest with the red series.

23 and 24 Communication spaces on the ground floor. The
    exposed fittings reflect the extreme austerity – both material
    and spiritual – of the Dominican lifestyle.

25 Opposite: Screen wall with *ondulatoires* opposite the refectory.
    The glass surfaces extending from floor to ceiling are
    segmented by concrete mullions that follow syncopated
    rhythms derived from the musical and mathematical
    compositions of Iannis Xenakis.

*'The architectural elements are light
and shade, walls and spaces.'*

26

27

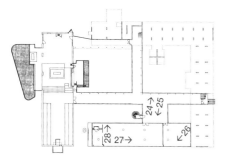

26 On the left, the door to the refectory and, on the right, the walkway to the church. The foreshortened entrance of the sun through the *ondulatoires* highlights the texture of the walls and casts shadows of the partitions onto the floor. The latter, made of untreated concrete, is laid in a grid pattern based on the Modulor. The effects achieved by this interaction illustrate Le Corbusier's declaration: 'I compose with light.'

27 Work and meeting room adjacent to the refectory; the *pans de verre* allow it to project boldly outwards.

28 and 29 General and partial view of the refectory. Unlike the individual rooms, collective areas such as the refectory are treated as open, continuous spaces to enhance communal life. The transparency of the screen wall on the two longer sides of the rectangle, fitted with *pans de verre*, ensures that sunlight enters uniformly, thereby uniting the space rather than creating any hierarchy.

30

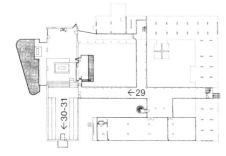

←29

←30-31

31

30 Opposite: Church entrance and the *pans de verre* wall
    shown earlier. This screen wall is transparent viewed from
    the front, but because the mullions are so close together,
    it appears more opaque when seen from an oblique angle.

31 Opposite: General view of the church from the altar. The
    starkness of the walls is intensified by their extraordinary
    height, and the vacuum created is intended to encourage
    contemplation. The diffuse lighting is meticulously
    calculated to mark out spaces and functions; the two strips
    on either side are intended to facilitate reading during the
    services. At the far end, the niche containing the organ.

32 Overhead light bleaches the wall by the organ before
    being engulfed in the corner shadows; as elsewhere in the
    monastery, the light depends on the position of the sun.

*'There are barely any light sources but they are well situated,
and this church, in its moving simplicity, awakens a feeling
of silence and contemplation.'*

33

34

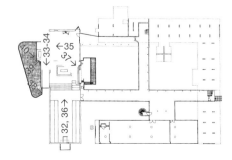

33 General view of the church, as seen from the organ area. At certain times of the day, the direct entrance of light through the slits heightens the effect of the colour scheme. In the centre background, the main altar, bounded by a side altar, to the left, and the sacristy, to the right.

34 Wall protecting the pit of the crypt. The theatricality of the bright yellow paint on the concrete is enhanced by the light pouring in through the three 'cannons of light', which are painted red, white and blue respectively. The dramatic name of these light sources accurately conveys their emotional impact.

35 and 36 Opposite: Detail of one of the cannons of light and the side altar, next to the wall by the pit of the crypt. The overhead light endows this space with a symbolic density that corroborates its essentially spiritual function.

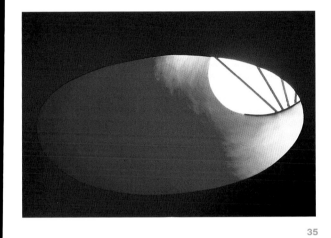

35

36

'The monks' church is important. It makes sense to me. It should induce powerful emotions by means of the play of proportions. As a fundamental sign of one of the most ancient of all institutions, the mass, the main altar is the supreme example of a sacred site and is the church's centre of gravity.'

37 Opposite: The main altar is located in the centre of the axes, on an unpolished slate floor in the highest area of the church.

38 The sacristy was designed as an independent volume – an approach common to much of Le Corbusier's work. A curved red plane is set amidst the church's orthogonal order, jutting out from the plane of the wall. The sunshine entering through the cannons of light – tapered openings aligned with the summer solstice – makes this element even more distinctive. The sacristy leads to the crypt, at the opposite end of the building. This journey involves going in the opposite direction around the sacristy, before descending, making a 180-degree turn and crossing the church under the ground to reach the small altars that form the crypt. This subterranean route, devoid of any guiding visual references, has a disorientating effect and gives a degree of abstraction to this part of the church.

39 Entrance to the crypt. The wall above forms a protective barrier marking the drop in the floor level compared to the church.

40 and 41 Views of the crypt, from either side. The small altars are set on a series of platforms that compensate for the gradient in this highly expressive space. Mortar was allowed to protrude through the wall to create interesting textures, which are heightened by the use of colour. The most spectacular effect, however, is supplied by the cannons of light, situated between the pit and the side altar, on the other side of the wall.

42

43

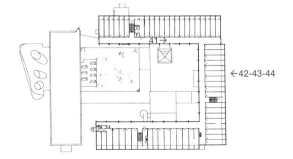

←42-43-44

42 Corridor, illuminated by the horizontal window strip on the opposite side, and the doors to the cells. Alongside each door are *aérateurs* – narrow vertical openings with pivoting wooden louvres – that allow air to pass through the cells.

43 Interior of a cell intended for temporary guests, but with the same characteristics as those of the monks. It is equipped only with elements essential to resting and working. In the background, the entrance to the balcony, which acts as a protective screen in extreme weather conditions.

44

45

44 The balcony frames a section of the magnificent
landscape of hills and trees that surrounds the monastery,
in contrast to the unremitting austerity of the small room.
The prefabricated modules that make up the balconies
are best appreciated from the interior; on the outside,
where they are incrusted with small stones, they have
a rougher appearance.

45 A small cupboard to hold bed linen separates the bed
from the washbasin set next to the door.

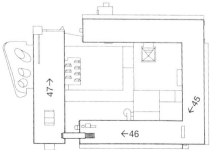

46 The roof terrace. In the foreground, the striking head of the stairwell. In the background, the steps that compensate for the gradient of the church, and the start of the walkway leading to it.

47 The steps, the walls protecting the walkway and the ventilation duct are all architectonic elements with a function that is not only visible but displayed in a dramatic fashion, because – apart from the top of the stairwell and the bell tower – they are virtually the only structures on view in this area. The exaggerated height of the perimeter walls deliberately obstructs the views from this perfect vantage point.

48 View of the bell tower from the roof of the church.

'Both the roof of the monastery and that of the church are covered with a thin layer of soil left to the devices of the wind, the birds and other transporters of seeds, to guarantee watertight and isothermal protection.'

kembs-niffer
lock

1962 haut-rhin

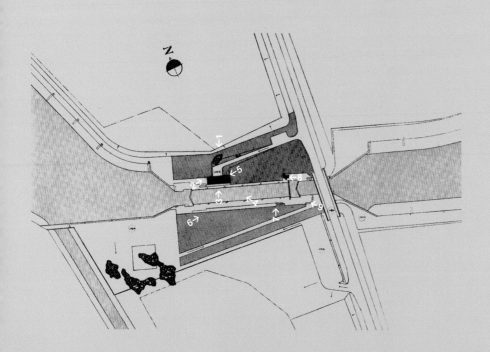

This lock, situated between Basel and Mulhouse, forms part of the canal connecting the Rhone with the Rhine. Le Corbusier built two of the elements that make up the complex: the customs building and the watchtower. Although these are closely related, they are independent structures clearly differentiated from each other: the horizontality of the block of customs offices and shipping facilities, running at a uniform height from the ground, allows it to integrate into the bare, open space and contrasts with the sculptural verticality of the tower.

Although the office building appears to be confined to this elevation above ground level, in fact it also stretches downwards to accommodate other spaces in the basement, including rooms used by the team in charge of the lock and areas reserved for heating equipment and other services.

This lower level – only visible from the other side of the canal – is reached by a flight of steps which adapts to, and compensates for, the gradient before leading to a cement staircase that climbs up to the ground floor. Two contrasting sloping planes cover the office block, appearing to split it in half – a perceptual division emphasized by a physical separation, in the form of an open passageway in the centre of the ground floor. This hollow roughly coincides with the meeting point of the two roof sections, thereby further accentuating the separation.

The juxtaposition of different planes, along with the stairs going down to the spaces in the basement, metaphorically recalls the change in water level created by a lock, so setting up a parallel between the architecture and its surroundings. A similar concept is apparent in another building featured here, the Heidi Weber Exhibition Pavilion, a posthumous work completed in 1967 in Zurich, where the parasol roof covers and protects the galleries.

Moreover, this effect is heightened in the customs building by the exposed drainpipes situated at both ends; these collect rainwater and send it into the ground, echoing the course of the water in the canal. This double function – utilitarian (drainage) and symbolic (evocation) – makes an important contribution to the overall impact of the building.

In contrast to the horizontality of the office building, visually accentuated by the single-height façade overlooking the lock, the vertical control tower soars up next to the lock gate, which is undoubtedly the main focus of the project, as it serves

to connect the two water flows. The double-faced top of the tower points towards both rivers at the same time, as it is twisted 45 degrees in relation to the tower's concrete base. Its function as a control tower is further enhanced by the unifying effect of the continuous glass wall.

As in the case of the customs building, a staircase serves as a linking element, running from the lowest part of the lock to its uppermost point, where it connects with the rising watchtower by means of the latter's own staircase, which rises to the rear and provides access to the highest space of all – the observation cabin.

As is customary in the work of Le Corbusier, the architecture on display in the Kembs-Niffer lock is faithful to the geometric rigour and disciplinary autonomy that he advocated, and so affirms its independence from the setting. This meticulous geometry, the fruit of painstaking calculation, is, however, a means and not an end itself; it neutralizes chaos and arbitrariness and is therefore always attentive and subordinate to the overriding creation of forms designed to create an emotional visual impact.

It could be said that the dialogue established with the site through metaphors that recall the functioning of the lock does not reflect a quest for mimesis but rather a desire for harmonious fusion based on the acknowledgment of differences. This is an essential characteristic of what has come to be known as modernist architecture. Le Corbusier himself cleared up the futile controversy about the nature of this project by stressing, between quotation marks, the essential meaning of his involvement:

'There is no longer any discussion as to whether this falls under architecture or engineering. It is a "constructed work". The administrators and engineers asked me to take part in their undertaking.' (1)

Source
(1) Le Corbusier, *The Complete Architectural Works, vol. 8, Last Works,* London, 1970, p. 46

1

2

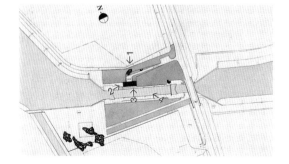

1 North façade, facing the canal. Taking advantage of the gradient, the basement is used to accommodate equipment and maintenance facilities. This area is linked by a staircase to the offices on the ground floor.

2 South façade, showing the front of the customs offices, which look out onto the canal but are protected from sunshine by the mullions and overhang.

3

4

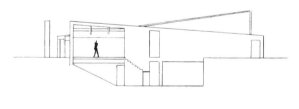

3   At the end of the office area, a corridor divides the ground-floor
    space, as well as providing access to both the staircase down
    to the basement and entrances to the various rooms. This
    division is accentuated by the corridor's location under the
    meeting point of the two roofs.

4   View of the customs and navigation building. The slope of the
    roofs directs the water to the huge drainpipe at one end, while
    also symbolizing the movement of the water in the lock.

5

6

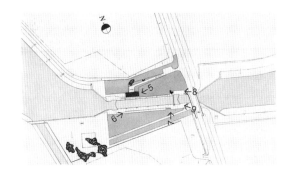

'There is no longer any discussion as to whether this falls under architecture or engineering. It is a "constructed work."'

5 Opposite: Detail of the drainpipe for rainwater running off the roof. This dramatic formal device echoes the lock's main function: the channelling of water from the Rhone to the Rhine. In the foreground, the chimney of the machine room in the basement.

6 View of the two architectural elements that comprise the lock complex: the customs building and the control tower.

7 The bold verticality of the control tower, set close to the lock gate, contrasts with the horizontal sweep of the customs building. The continuous glass of the cabin on the top bears witness to the tower's function of watching over the two waterways; the cabin is twisted so that each face looks onto both rivers. The lower volumes house machinery.

8   Opposite: To the rear of the control tower, a staircase provides access to the various levels. With the same metaphorical intent as some other elements already described – the staircase that spans the distance between the basement and ground floor, the drainpipes under the roofs – this staircase also recalls the movement of the water through the lock, as well as serving its obvious utilitarian purpose.

9   View of the complex, with the lock gate in the foreground and the customs building in the background. The steps that rise from the lower level of the lock to ground level face the observatory, and their ascent can be continued visually by means of the stairs on the tower. This device serves to link the function of the lock gate, the key element of the complex, with the control tower. This network of metaphors sets up a dialogue that integrates the architecture with its setting, while avoiding any mimesis that would jeopardize the building's autonomy.

heidi weber
exhibition pavilion
(la maison de l'homme) 1963–67 zurich

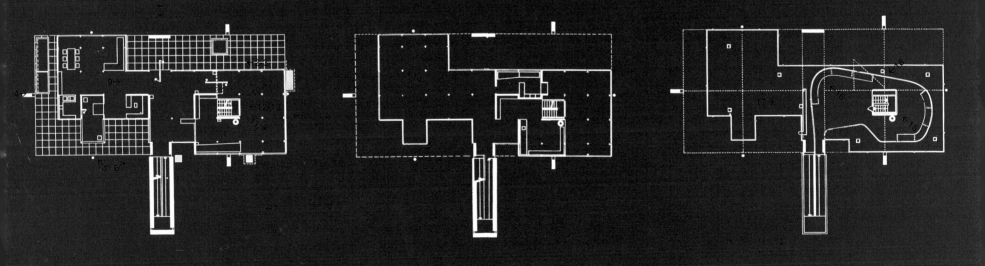

'*This is a showcase house to be built for Mme Heidi Weber in the park in Zurich. This house must serve the double function of museum-house and gallery-house devoted to the public display of Le Corbusier's pictorial and sculptural work, his published works and graphic art: lithographs, prints, etc.*' (1)

The pavilion, commissioned by the art dealer Heidi Weber (who specialized in the promotion of Le Corbusier's artworks) and built beside a lake in the Zurichhorn Park, was never planned as a residence for its owner. Even though it contains a kitchen, bathroom and bedroom, this building should be understood as a setting in which artists – including Le Corbusier himself – could create and exhibit their work. The name by which it would later be known, *La Maison de l'Homme*, emphasizes the architect's underlying desire to design a space adapted to the human scale, as reflected in a passage from the *Oeuvre complète*:

'*Both the architecture and the artworks must be shown on the modest scale of a nomadic dwelling, with its measurements on a 'human scale', thus avoiding the feeling of arbitrariness found in so-called "art galleries".*' (2)

This recalls Le Corbusier's criticism of the exorbitant difference in the scale of the exhibition space and the works on display in the Musée National de l'Art Moderne in Paris; he believed that what ought to be a suitable framework for enhancing the expressivity of an artwork in fact had the effect of dulling the desired emotional impact on the spectator.

The pavilion opened in 1967, two years after Le Corbusier's death. It is therefore one of his posthumous works, but the project's most direct and formally recognizable precedents are his design for the exhibition 'Synthèse des arts majeurs', held in Porte Maillot, Paris, in 1950, and in the National Museum of Western Art, Tokyo (1957–59). Its earliest reference points, however, can be found in two more distant dates: 1928, when Le Corbusier designed a temporary pavilion with a metal structure for Nestlé, as part of a trade fair in Paris; and 1939, when he drew up the 'Saison de l'eau' project for an exhibition in Liège.

Le Corbusier, sketch for National Museum of Western Art, Tokyo, 1957

Le Corbusier, sketch for exhibition in Liège, 1939

Before this building was finally put up in Zurich, there had been two frustrated attempts to bring it to fruition: the project for the Ahrenberg exhibition pavilion in Stockholm in 1962 and, the following year, the project for the Erlenbach International Art Centre in Frankfurt. So, the Heidi Weber Pavilion is the culmination of a series of experiments that stretched across much of Le Corbusier's career, illustrating, once again, his persistent drive, the considered maturity of his ideas and his firm belief in his findings.

The pavilion comprises three elements that are imbued with great independence and formal autonomy: the roof, the interior volume and the ramp. These clearly differentiated components reflect the functional flexibility required of the pavilion.

The roof is made up of a complex structure of steel spokes that form a protective parasol covering the cube-shaped interior modules.

'*The roof as brise-soleil was positioned first. The "inhabitable structure" was built afterwards, under cover (sheltered from rain, etc.).*' (3)

This parasol is divided into two metal sheets, each with a square outline but folded in different directions – one upwards and one downwards; these sheets are supported by hollow columns with rectangular bases and steel tubes that mark the building's two axes. The formal boldness and dynamism of the roof's sloping planes contrast strongly with the modular and geometric uniformity of the galleries themselves. At the same time, the placement of the roof supports, running from the parasol's vertices to its central points, sets bounds on the otherwise seemingly unlimited growth suggested by the cubes.

One of the roof supports coincides with the centre of the pavilion's entrance, creating an interference that is not so much spatial and physical but rather perceptual. In this respect, Deborah Gans, in her *Le Corbusier Guide* (4), points out the resemblance between the entrance to the pavilion and the entrance to the Villa Savoye. In effect, both buildings involve a similar opposition between the grid of exterior and interior columns. Once the threshold is crossed, the reference of the central exterior column disappears or, to be more precise, the latter is divided into two side pieces that frame the doorway.

Furthermore, the cellular configuration of the interior volume takes the form of a mesh, with modules defined by a 226-cm (89-in) length based on the measurement unit of the Modulor – the height reached by a man 182 cm (6 ft) tall with his arm stretched upwards. The façades are closed off by strips of glass or enamelled panels in bright, primary colours. The top of the cubes forms a surface underneath the parasol on which visitors can walk and enjoy the expansive views.

In this project, Le Corbusier applied the system known as Le Brevet ('The Patent') or 226 x 226 x 226, which he had been experimenting with since 1949 and which had made an appearance in his two studies for the 'Roq' and 'Rob' project in Cap Martin, on the French Riviera. His interest in alveolar volumes as a system with many possible combinations and great flexibility also had an important precedent in earlier experiments with light panels undertaken by Jean Prouvé.

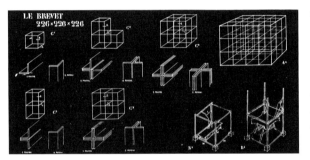

Le Corbusier, diagram showing the principle of Le Brevet

'The first idea for alveolar volumes dates back to 1950, when Jean Prouvé's beams of folded metal sheets were installed in the Unité in Marseilles. These offered notable benefits in terms of their lightness, transportation and fitting.' (5)

The sharp outlines of the cubes are set off by the planes of glass and metal on the faces that define them. The exquisite technical sophistication of these surfaces contrasts strikingly with Le Corbusier's previous work, dominated by the emphatic rawness of concrete.

Even so, concrete was used once again in this posthumous work for the pavilion's third component, the ramp, set perpendicular to the main floor of the interior cube-shaped volume. Its spatial configuration, along with its physical appearance and texture – reminiscent of a sturdy wall – allow the ramp to serve a dual communicative function, as it is both a mass that links the various interior spaces vertically and a form that mediates between the pavilion's metallic fragility and the surrounding natural landscape. Apart from the pavilion's base and the sculptural interior staircase, this ramp is the only element made of concrete.

The pavilion would fulfil its programmatic objectives by exhibiting Le Corbusier's artistic experiments in its galleries, along with the work of other artists. This commitment to the avant-garde would, however, be deepened and consolidated by a social commitment focusing on emerging problems associated with housing, thereby creating a metaphor for the social awareness inherent in Le Corbusier's own work.

'In 1969 I created a FORUM ON ENVIRONMENTAL PROBLEMS in the Centre Le Corbusier. In the pavilion I primarily held exhibitions with critical discourses that helped to resolve problems associated with today's living conditions. Through this, I succeeded in raising public interest in issues related to our environment.' (6)

Sources
(1) Le Corbusier, *The Complete Architectural Works, vol. 7, 1957–1965,* London, 1970, p. 22
(2) Le Corbusier, *The Complete Architectural Works, vol. 7, 1957–1965,* p. 22
(3) Le Corbusier, *The Complete Architectural Works, vol. 8, Last Works*, London, 1970, p. 148
(4) Deborah Gans, *The Le Corbusier Guide*, New York, 1987
(5) Le Corbusier, *Le Modulor et Le Modulor 2*, Basel, 2000
(6) Heidi Weber, *LC ZCH. Plans and Photographs*, Heidi Weber Exhibitions Pavilion, Zurich, undated

1   South façade, facing the Zurichhorn Park and close to the
      lake. Two of the three elements that define the pavilion are
      clearly seen: the roof – with a structure of steel spokes and
      a parasol of sloping sheets of metal – and the modular
      volume below it. The roof is supported by columns and steel
      tubes that mark the meeting points of its sloping panels.
      One half of the roof points upwards, the other downwards.
      In contrast to the sculptural distinctiveness of the roof, the
      modular structure of the internal volume demonstrates an
      egalitarian and uniform approach to space.

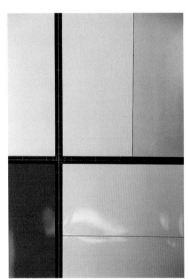

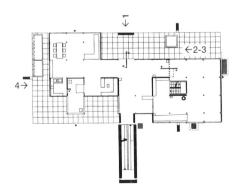

2

3

2 Opposite: Detail of the enamelled panels that enclose the exhibition spaces.

3 Opposite: Partial view of the south face, showing the pivoting door in the centre of the façade that leads to the exhibition spaces inside.

4 East façade. As in the case of the other façades, the supports are set at the end of the roof, in the centre, curbing the seemingly unrestricted capacity for growth suggested by the pavilion's cube-shaped forms.

5

6

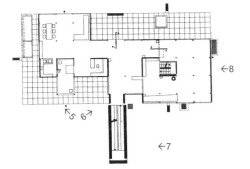

←8

←5 6→

←7

5   Main entrance to the pavilion, on the north façade. The access area protrudes outwards, with an empty space below indicating the way in. The way is blocked by the tubular support in front, which is echoed by the two thin supports under the cube.

6   Meeting point of the ramp and the pavilion.

7   Opposite: The ramp – the third defining element of this building – is situated on the north side and connects the different levels of the pavilion. Its striking placement – outside the exhibition area – and the material used – exposed concrete – heightens the sharp contrast with both the taut geometry of the building and its natural surroundings.

8   West façade, consisting entirely of enamelled panels. The vivid primary colours enliven the otherwise neutral modular formation. Conversely, the striking forms of the roof are offset by its uniform, neutral colour.

7

8

'The principal connection between the floors – besides a narrow stairway –
is the ramp. It is also clearly "legible" in the external design of the house.'

9

10

11

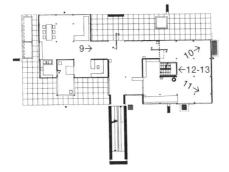

9, 10 and 11 Views of the ground floor of the pavilion. The long corridor running parallel to the south façade leads to the larger, double-height hall, which clearly illustrates the building's cellular composition, based on the measurement unit of the Modulor (226 cm/89 in), the height reached by a man 182 cm (6 ft) tall with his arm extended upwards. The system applied, known as *Le Brevet* or 226 x 226 x 226, had already been used by Le Corbusier in earlier experimental works. The glass wall and enamelled panels and the metal pillars dotted around the space convey the mesh-like concept of the pavilion.

12 and 13 Opposite: This hall is connected to the first floor via a concrete staircase – the only element, apart from the ramp, built on the ground with this material.

'In the centre, the red heating chimney and, right, the concrete stairway.'

14

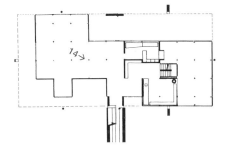

'Both the architecture and the artworks must be shown on the modest scale of a nomadic dwelling, with its measurements on a "human scale", thus avoiding the feeling of arbitrariness found in so-called "art galleries".'

14 Opposite: First floor. The low height of the ceiling focuses the attention on the exhibited artworks. As on the ground floor, the Modulor system is highlighted by the changing colour of the outlines, whose sharp edges and clean, delicate finishes contrast markedly with the rough concrete used in Le Corbusier's earlier works.

15 The upper level on top of the cubes forms a space beneath the sloping sheet metal of the parasol. This area serves as a vantage point for the park and a relaxation area; it also permits close inspection of the plates comprising the metal canopy, whose changes in plane both enrich and frame the setting. In the foreground, the lift shaft.

16

17

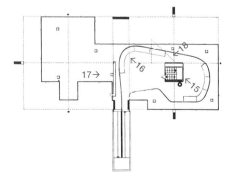

'The roof as brise-soleil was positioned first.
The "inhabitable structure" was built afterwards,
under cover (sheltered from rain, etc.).'

16 and 17 Opposite: Two views of the top surface, showing
the different approaches to the floor and the roof: the
predominantly curved forms of the former and the
horizontality of the seating elements contrast with
the rectilinear obliqueness of the parasol overhead.

18 This opening in the folded metal of the parasol is a
simple geometric form that frees and prolongs the gaze:
'The triangle of the roof opening towards the sky'.

Sources of quotations

Page 13

Jean Jenger (ed.), *Le Corbusier. Choix de lettres*, Basel, 2002, p. 40

Page 32

Le Corbusier, *Vers une architecture*, Paris, 1923

Page 33

Le Corbusier, *Vers une architecture*, p. 62

Page 39

Le Corbusier, *Une petite maison*, Basel, 2001, p. 17

Page 43

Le Corbusier, *Précisions sur un état présent de l'architecture et l'urbanisme*, Paris, 1960

Page 47

Le Corbusier, *The Complete Architectural Works, vol. 1, 1910–1929*, London, 1964, p. 74

Page 49

Le Corbusier, *Une petite maison*, p. 26

Page 50

Le Corbusier, *Une petite maison*, p. 28

Page 51

Le Corbusier, *Une petite maison*, p. 21

Page 53

Le Corbusier, *Une petite maison*, p. 45

Page 59

Le Corbusier, *Précisions sur un état présent de l'architecture et l'urbanisme*, p. 158

Page 62

Le Corbusier, *Précisions sur un état présent de l'architecture et l'urbanisme,* p. 158

Page 63

Le Corbusier, *The Complete Architectural Works, vol. 2, 1929–1934*, London, 1964, p. 25

Page 68

Le Corbusier, *Précisions sur un état présent de l'architecture et l'urbanisme*, p. 158

Page 73

Le Corbusier, *The Complete Architectural Works, vol. 2, 1929–1934*, London, 1964, p. 29

Page 75

Le Corbusier, *Précisions sur un état présent de l'architecture et l'urbanisme*, p. 158

Page 89

Le Corbusier, *The Complete Architectural Works, vol. 2, 1929–1934*, London, 1964, p. 85

Page 93

Le Corbusier, *The Complete Architectural Works, vol. 2, 1929–1934*, London, 1964, p. 79

Page 99

Le Corbusier, *Le Modulor et Le Modulor 2*, Basel, 2000

Page 103

Jean Jenger (ed.), *Le Corbusier. Choix de lettres*, p. 333

Page 117
Le Corbusier, *The Complete Architectural Works, vol. 5, 1946–1952*, London, 1970, p. 194

Page 119
Le Corbusier, *The Complete Architectural Works, vol. 5, 1946–1952*, London, 1970, p. 199

Page 121
Le Corbusier, *The Complete Architectural Works, vol. 5, 1946–1952*, London, 1970, p. 204

Page 122
Le Corbusier, *The Complete Architectural Works, vol. 5, 1946–1952*, London, 1970, p. 205

Page 127
Le Corbusier, *The Complete Architectural Works, vol. 5, 1946–1952*, London, 1970, p. 205

Page 131
Le Corbusier, *The Complete Architectural Works, vol. 5, 1946–1952*, London, 1970, p. 194

Page 133
Le Corbusier, *The Complete Architectural Works, vol. 5, 1946–1952*, London, 1970, p. 221

Page 134
Le Corbusier, *Vers un architecture*, p. 16

Page 143
Jean Petit, *Un couvent de Le Corbusier*, Paris, 2001, p. 20

Page 148
Jean Petit, *Un couvent de Le Corbusier*, p. 8

Page 150
Le Corbusier, *Vers une architecture,* p. 22

Page 155
Le Corbusier, *The Complete Architectural Works, vol. 7, 1957–1965,* London, 1970, p. 49

Page 158
Jean Petit, *Un couvent de Le Corbusier*, p. 20

Page 165
Jean Petit, *Un couvent de Le Corbusier*, p. 111

Page 170
Le Corbusier, *The Complete Architectural Works, vol. 8, Last Works,* London, 1970, p. 48

Page 181
Le Corbusier, *The Complete Architectural Works, vol. 8, Last Works,* London, 1970, p. 142

Page 183
Le Corbusier, *The Complete Architectural Works, vol. 8, Last Works,* London, 1970, p. 152

Page 184
Le Corbusier, *The Complete Architectural Works, vol. 7, 1957–1965,* London, 1970, p. 22

Page 186
Le Corbusier, *The Complete Architectural Works, vol. 8, Last Works,* London, 1970, p. 148

Index